PHOT⊙SHOP

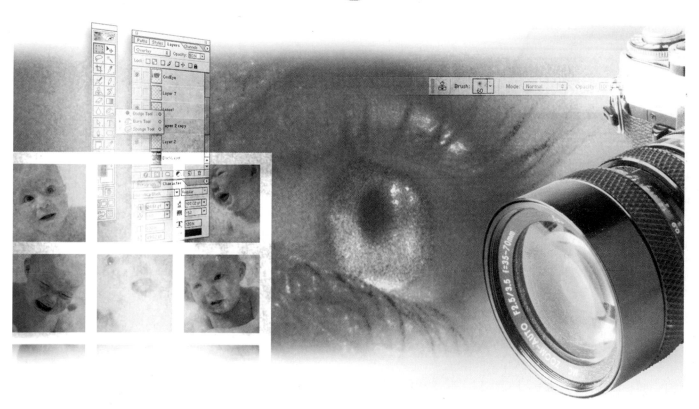

PHOTO-RETOUCHING SECRETS

BY SCOTT KELBY

The Adobe® Photoshop® 6
Photo-Retouching Secrets
Team

PRODUCTION EDITOR
Chris Main

COPY EDITOR
Barbara Thompson

TYPE TWEAKING
Dave Damstra

CREATIVE DIRECTOR
AND COVER DESIGN
Felix Nelson

STOCK IMAGES
The stock images in this book
are courtesy of PhotoDisc,
www.photodisc.com

PUBLISHED BY
New Riders Publishing

Copyright © 2001 by New Riders Publishing

FIRST EDITION: May, 2001

International Standard Book Number: 0-7357-1146-1

Library of Congress Catalog Card Number: 00-108793

05 04 03 02 01   7 6 5 4 3 2 1

Interpretation of the printing code: The rightmost double-digit number is the year of the book's printing; the rightmost single-digit number is the number of the book's printing. For example, the printing code 01-1 shows that the first printing of the book occurred in 2001.

Composed in Myriad and Minion by New Riders Publishing

Printed in the United States of America

Trademarks

Warning and Disclaimer

This book
is dedicated
to my
son Jordan,
who I firmly
believe
is the single,
greatest
little boy
in the
world.

ACKNOWLEDGMENTS

I have so many wonderful people to thank for their help with this book, that once I list them all, you're going to ponder if I really did anything at all.

First, I want to thank my amazing wife Kalebra. Anyone who knows her, knows how much she is a part of everything I do, and everything I am. Without her by my side, there's no reason to do any of it. They say that if you have a great marriage, it's like being married to your very best friend in the world, and after 12 years, I can tell you that's absolutely true.

Kalebra has been blessed with many special gifts. One of her secret super powers is her uncanny ability to find and assemble the most creative, good-natured, honest, hardworking, and fun people into a dream team that can tackle any project. Thanks to her, I'm privileged to have the chance to work with people like Chris Main, an absolutely kick-butt editor and project manager who always keeps his cool, no matter how close the deadlines loom; Felix Nelson, a creative director who totally "gets it," and calling him a creative director doesn't give credit for all the ways he has touched this book and our company as a whole; and Dave Damstra, "The Michigan Layout Machine," who keeps crankin' out those squeaky-clean "Damstrasized" pages at the speed of three men. They are, hands down, the best team I've ever worked with, and I'd put Chris, Felix, and Dave up against any team in the business. I can't thank them enough for everything they do, and I wouldn't attempt a book like this without them.

I want to express my deep gratitude to my friends and business partners Jim Workman and Jean A. Kendra for their patience, feedback, and belief in the project from start to finish. It's great to have partners who really believe in you, and that makes my job much easier and infinitely more enjoyable.

I want to thank my brother Jeff Kelby for his constant support, and for keeping me rolling in the aisles at work. I want to thank Julie Stephenson, who takes over after the book is printed and makes sure everything runs smoothly on the publishing and fulfillment end. I'm also grateful to my top-notch customer service team, Tameka Thomas, Maureen Arms, Amanda McCormack, Anna Fracassi, Barbara Daniels, and Sandureen Stoker, who make it happen every day. I want to thank Lawrence Atkinson and Mike Donadio for the great job they do in keeping everything moving out the doors on time. I want to thank Dave Moser for his reservoir of enthusiasm, his unwavering commitment to quality, and for making sure I had the time I needed to finish this book. I want to thank Barbara Thompson for joining our team and keeping all our other projects moving forward while I was working on the book. I want to thank the amazing Allison Hagenbuckle, my assistant, for keeping me focused and making sure I'm doing what I'm supposed to be doing, when I'm supposed to be doing it. Thanks to Ronni "Miss Ronni" O'Neil for all her help and for being a part of our team. Also, thanks to Chris Smith and Scott Stahley for "keepin' it real!"

I also want to thank Julieanne Kost, Russell Preston Brown, Jim DiVitale, Helene DeLillo, Jim Patterson, Doug Gornick, Manuel Obordo, Robb Kerr, and all the other Photoshop experts who over the years have shared their retouching techniques and helped to make this book far better than it ever would have been. Thanks to my friends at Adobe Systems: Barbara Rice, Kevin Connor, Karen Gauthier, Jill Nakashima, Susan Doering, Terry White, and Rye Livingston.

I am indebted to all my mentors whose whip-cracking and wisdom have touched every aspect of my life: John Graden, Dave Gales, Jim Lemmin, and my wonderful brother Jeff. I would like to thank my dad Jerry Kelby for being the dad all other dads are measured by.

And lastly, an extra special thanks goes to my wonderful little boy Jordan, who patiently sat with me many a night, cuddled up on the couch, while I wrote this book on my PowerBook. Just seeing him reminds me every day of why God put me on this earth, and how blessed I am that He brought my wife and I together those many years ago.

ABOUT THE AUTHOR

Scott Kelby

 Scott is editor in chief of *Photoshop User* magazine and president of the National Association of Photoshop Professionals, the trade association for Adobe® Photoshop® users. Scott is also editor in chief of *Mac Design Magazine*, a print magazine for Macintosh graphic designers, and president and CEO of KW Media Group, Inc., a Florida-based graphics training and publishing firm.

Scott is author of the book *Photoshop 6.0 Down & Dirty Tricks,* from NAPP Publishing, and a contributing author to the books, *Photoshop 6 Effects Magic* from New Riders, *Maclopedia, the Ultimate Reference on Everything Macintosh* from Hayden Books, and *Adobe Web Design and Publishing Unleashed* from Sams.net Publishing.

Scott is an Adobe Certified Expert (ACE) in Photoshop, training director for the Adobe Photoshop Seminar Tour, Technical Chair and Educational Director of PhotoshopWorld (the annual convention for Adobe Photoshop users), and he is a speaker at graphics trade shows and events around the world. Scott is also featured in a series of Photoshop, Illustrator, and Web design video training tapes and has been training graphics professionals across the country since 1993.

Scott lives in the Tampa Bay area of Florida with his wife Kalebra and his 4-year-old son Jordan. For more background info visit www.scottkelby.com.

TABLE OF CONTENTS

TABLE OF CONTENTS

INTRODUCTION

Why I wrote this book

The inspiration for this book came from a number of different sources. First and foremost, I wanted to expand upon my Photoshop training video *Photoshop Photo-Retouching Techniques*. This has been one of my best-selling videos for years, but because it was only 60 minutes in length, I could only cover a small portion of the cool retouching techniques I'd learned from some of the best in the business. I had considered releasing other videos to create a series of tapes, but then, even if we continued to charge only $39.95 per video, with two or three videos in the series, you're looking at nearly $120, and that would put the training out of reach for many people who really could get a lot out of it.

Secondly, I wanted to expand upon my live photo-retouching session that I do with the Adobe Photoshop Seminar Tour. It's often the most popular session of the day, but again, I'm limited to 60 minutes max, and that's just not enough time. There are just too many tricks I want to share!

The third reason I wanted to create this book was to fulfill the requests from readers of my previous book, *Photoshop 6.0 Down & Dirty Tricks*. So many people write in and say, "You need to do a book on photo retouching, but make it just like your *Down & Dirty Tricks* book, with everything step-by-step, simple, and to the point" that I felt I already had an audience for the book.

There's a fourth reason: I love doing this! I love teaching Photoshop. Writing books, doing videos, writing magazine columns—I think it's a blast, and this book is a culmination of my live retouching classes, my retouching video, articles I've written in *Photoshop User* magazine, and some of the new retouching techniques that I'm writing about for the first time in this book.

Here's how I feel about it: It took me a long time to learn these techniques, because very few people were willing to share "the tricks of the trade" with me. They were so concerned with protecting what they had learned that they wouldn't give that info to anyone. I guess they felt that if they gave away all of their secrets, it would make them less valuable. I feel exactly the opposite. I feel like it's my duty, even an honor, to share these techniques so that anyone who wants to can learn them and pass them on to others. I believe learning Photoshop shouldn't be tedious, complicated, and confusing. I feel it should be exciting, fascinating, and always, without exception, fun. And the better you know Photoshop, the more fun you'll have. That's what this book is all about.

Is this book for me?

That depends. Do you have $39.95? (Kidding!) Actually, it's very important to me that the people who spend their hard-earned money on this book, get more than their money's worth. The best way for me to reach that goal is to try and make sure that the people who buy this book are the people for whom I expressly wrote this book.

This book (and all my books) are written specifically for people who want to learn "the funk and not the junk." This book is not a master class on photo retouching. It's not an "experts-only" book. It's not a book on high-end advanced techniques that requires years of experience to really take advantage of what it teaches. Rather, this is a "down and dirty, get the job done fast, use all the shortcuts and tricks, and, most importantly, have a great time while you're doing it" book. What I think you'll really like about this book is that you'll be able to do all the techniques you find in this book. All of them. Every one. This isn't the hard stuff, it's the fun stuff—the stuff that puts a smile on your face when you start using it yourself.

At the end of the day, this is what it comes down to: You're really the best judge whether this book is for you (but I can help lead you in the right direction, right?). This book is for you if you're one of those people looking for the fastest, easiest way possible to learn retouching, without a lot of jargon or assumptions that you're already a Photoshop expert, so you can start retouching and repairing photos *today*. If that sounds like you, then this book *is* for you.

However, this book isn't for everybody (internal note to editor: please don't tell my publisher that I wrote that). If you're looking for a retouching book that has detailed discussions of pixels, resolution, file formats, color management, and an in-depth look into the art of high-end photo retouching, this isn't for you. (Remember, if you determine that this book is not for you, certainly you know somebody that it's ideal for, so don't hesitate to buy them a copy. Or two. Hey, I still have to pay the bills.)

This book is for you if you're one of those people looking for the fastest, easiest way possible to learn retouching... so you can start retouching and repairing photos today.

Cutting to the chase

In my *Down & Dirty Tricks* book, I didn't want it to read like a novel, where you have to start at Chapter One and read chapter by chapter so you don't get lost in the story. I designed it more like an effects cookbook so you could jump to anyplace in the book and create the effect, regardless of your experience in Photoshop. That worked so well, I wanted to repeat that concept in this book, but there's one little twist. You can jump to any page and start doing the techniques, but if you're new to retouching and you haven't used the Clone Stamp tool (often called the Rubber Stamp tool), then I really recommend that you read the first technique in Chapter One, "Basic Cloning with the Clone Stamp Tool" (it's just four pages), and then you can jump in anywhere and start retouching. Go right to the chapters and techniques that interest you most. They don't get harder or more detailed near the end of the book, so find the techniques you want to learn and start there.

Also, like my previous book, I spell everything out. So if you've been using Photoshop for years, don't let it put you off because instead of just writing "create a new layer," I usually write, "create a new layer by clicking on the New Layer icon at the bottom of the Layers palette." I do that because I want everyone, at any skill level, to be able to open the book to any page and start retouching.

Most Photoshop books start off with a few chapters that explain the Photoshop basics—how to use the tools, etc., but I didn't. Most retouching books would start with a detailed explanation of what cloning is, then it would examine every option for the tool, explain the different cloning techniques, etc., but again, I didn't include that chapter either. I couldn't wait to get right to the tricks, so I did, right in Chapter One.

I figured that (a) if you read the first technique and spent just two minutes with the tool, it would become pretty obvious how it works, and (b) if you wanted one of those "tell me everything before I do anything" books, that's what you would have bought.

How to use this book

This is a book you want to read at your computer. Do not attempt to read it while driving a motor vehicle or operating heavy machinery. That's because you'll only wind up going back home, starting up your computer, and launching Photoshop to try out all your new tricks. So you might as well be in front of your computer before you read the first chapter. You may find it helpful to bring along some provisions, in case you wind up sitting there for days, retouching every damaged image you can get your hands on (hey… it could happen).

Can I get the images used in the book?

Although the whole idea behind this book is for you to apply these retouching techniques on your own images, you can practice on some of the same images that are used in this book by downloading the low-res JPEG versions from the book's companion Web site at **www.photoretouchingsecrets.com**. A number of the images available for download are courtesy of royalty-free stock image provider PhotoDisc (www.photodisc.com). I've been a fan of PhotoDisc since they arrived on the scene years ago, when they changed the face of the stock image market forever with their high-quality images and groundbreaking price structure. I can't thank them enough for making some of their images used in the book available for download from the book's site. Most of the vintage, damaged, ripped, bent, scotch-taped, and otherwise traumatized photos are courtesy of my good friend and business partner Jim Workman. Jim has a huge collection of images that he and his family apparently had no plan of preserving for future generations to enjoy, and the resulting damage made them ideal for retouching projects in this book.

Is this book for Macintosh, PC, or both?

It's for both, because (luckily for me) Photoshop is identical on both the Macintosh and PC platforms. However, even though the software is the same, the keyboards on the Mac and PC are slightly different. There are actually just three keys that have different names on a Mac keyboard when compared with a PC keyboard, so every time I give a keyboard shortcut, I give both the Macintosh and PC keyboard shortcuts. See, I care. (By the way, the three keys are Command, Option, Control on the Mac and Control, Alt, Right-click respectively on the PC.)

Are we ready yet?

Yes, grasshopper, you are now ready to begin. As always, to become one with the retouch, we must follow the path that leads to retouching enlightenment. First, don the sacred retouching robe, then begin the chant we taught in Chapter Eleven. If you haven't shaved your head yet, you may still begin, but start with Chapter Thirteen, which is titled "I don't deserve to retouch photos for I have not yet shaved my head." OK, I admit it—none of that is really in the book, but if it had been, I surely would've raised the cover price (kidding). So dim the lights, put *Barry White's Greatest Hits* on the stereo, and begin to unlock a world of Photoshop retouching delights that dare not speak its name.

You've come this far. I'm Impressed

Thanks for taking the time to read this introduction (nobody reads introductions any more. That's why I could sneak that "don the sacred robe" stuff in), and for giving me the opportunity to teach you some of my favorite Photoshop Photo-Retouching Secrets.

Most Photoshop books start off with a few chapters that explain the Photoshop basics—how to use the tools, etc., but I didn't….I couldn't wait to get right to the tricks…

As you might imagine, any book on Photoshop retouching is going to spend a significant amount of time on the

Send in the Clones
cloning tips and techniques

Rubber Stamp tool. That's why my original title for this chapter was "Rubber Soul," named after a classic album by either the Beatles or Britney Spears (I can't remember which). But in Photoshop® 6.0, Adobe® changed the name of the tool from the Rubber Stamp tool to the Clone Stamp tool. Since the word "Rubber" was gone, so was my cool "Rubber Soul" chapter title. I quietly sobbed for days.

Rather than explaining all the nuances of the Rubber Stamp (pardon me, Clone Stamp) tool, I figured you'd rather learn it by doing it. So on the next four pages, you'll find a quick project that will have you using, and understanding, the tool in just minutes. But once you learn to clone, be careful. The last guys who learned the secret of cloning wound up in a laboratory in England, cloning things that raised a lot of ethical questions (but they did end up with some lovely winter coats).

Basic Cloning with the Clone Stamp Tool

Since this is a retouching book, you'd better start out by learning how to use the Rubber Stamp tool. (OK, In Photoshop 6.0, the official name for the tool is the "Clone Stamp Tool," but outside the walls of Adobe's headquarters, just about everybody still calls it the "Rubber Stamp tool," since its icon looks like a rubber stamp.)

STEP ONE: Cloning is a technique that enables you to pick an object within your image and repeat it (or clone it) to another area in your image using a brush. This technique is not just used for adding more objects; it can also be used for deleting objects from images, so it's an important technique to learn right from the beginning. You can start this cloning technique by opening an image that contains an object you want to clone (in the example we're using here, we're going to add another set of power lines between the two existing sets).

STEP TWO: Press the letter "s" to get the Clone Stamp tool (from here on out, I'm calling it the Rubber Stamp tool). Once you've got it, you can choose which kind of tip you want on your brush (hard-edged, soft-edged, etc.) from the Brushes pop-down menu, found in the Options Bar (it's just below the Menu bar at the top of your screen). If you look up in the left side, you'll see the word "Brush" and a thumbnail image of your current brush tip. To choose a different brush, click on the down-facing triangle to the immediate right of the brush thumbnail and a pop-down menu will appear where you can choose your desired brush. For this tutorial, choose the soft-edged brush with a 45 under it (that's a 45-pixel sized brush).

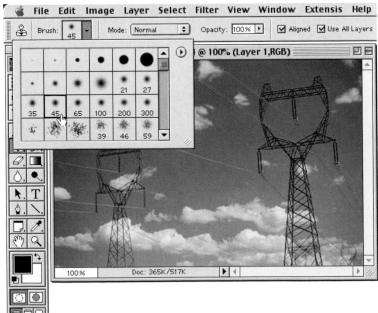

STEP THREE: Position your cursor over the object you want to repeat (or clone) to another area within your image. Hold the Option key (PC: Alt key) and click once on the area you want to clone. In the example at left, I'm clicking directly on the center of the right-hand tower (highlighted in the image at left). When you do this, you'll see a cursor icon appear that looks like a rubber stamp. By Option-clicking (PC: Alt-clicking) on this spot, you're telling Photoshop, "This is what I want to clone." That area is now set as the starting point for your Rubber Stamp to clone *from*.

STEP FOUR: Now that you've defined what you want to clone (incidentally, that process is called "sampling"), move your cursor to the area within your image where you want your cloned image to appear (in this example, where you want your cloned tower to appear). I wanted my cloned tower to appear to the left of the original tower, so I moved my cursor to the area between the two towers.

QUICK TIPS

To change the size of your brush, press the left bracket ([) key on your keyboard to make the brush smaller and the right bracket (]) key to make the brush larger.

STEP FIVE: Now, click the mouse button and begin to paint. As you paint, you'll now notice there are two cursors on the screen. The cursor that looks like a crosshair (✛) shows where you're cloning *"from"* (the spot where you Option/Alt-clicked), and the circular brush cursor shows where you're cloning *"to."* As you paint, the original tower will start to paint in as well. Think of it like this: Instead of dipping your brush into a paint can filled with color (such as blue or red), you're dipping your brush into a paint can filled with power lines, and when you paint, instead of color, you get power lines. If that sounds crazy, it should.

STEP SIX: Continue painting (cloning) in the power line. Be careful not to let your brush accidentally paint over the original power lines—stop just before you reach the edge of it. While you're doing this, you have to keep an eye on both the cursor you're painting with and the cursor where you're painting (sampling) from, because it's very easy to let the crosshair (that shows where you're sampling from), stray onto other parts of your image.

STEP SEVEN: Besides accidentally picking up parts of the original tower, if you reach the edge of your image, you'll encounter another problem—you'll start painting a hard edge (as shown here). If this happens, press Command-Z (PC: Control-Z) to undo your last step and try again. Because you're likely to make a few mistakes at first, only clone small areas and release the mouse button. If it looks OK, start painting again and you'll pick up right where you left off, because, unless you "resample" in a different location by Option/Alt-clicking, Photoshop remembers where you sampled earlier, so it's very easy to stop and restart when cloning like this.

STEP EIGHT: Continue painting (cloning) until the object you want to add is complete. If you want to add another tower to this image, perhaps one of the smaller ones behind the original in the distance, you could resample directly on the tiny tower in the lower right-hand corner. Do this by Option-clicking (PC: Alt-clicking) once on the tower, then move your cursor to the left until you're between the two towers and begin painting.

Every time you clone, it's the same three-step pattern: (1) Sample the object you want to clone by Option/Alt-clicking, (2) move to a new area, and (3) start painting. As you move through this chapter and the rest of the book, you'll learn other cloning techniques, and we'll use some of the Rubber Stamp tool's options (which appear in the Options Bar) to expand its range of use. But for now, if you understand how to perform this basic cloning technique, the rest is pretty easy.

Cloning away Unwanted Objects in Your Image

As useful as the Rubber Stamp tool is for replicating (cloning) objects within your image, it is probably used more often for removing objects from your image that you don't want. For this tutorial, we're going to combine the Rubber Stamp tool with some other techniques that you'll find really helpful in removing objects from existing images.

STEP ONE: In this instance, we have an image with a young woman sitting on the grass leaning against a fence in front of a barn. The problem with this photo is that we need to use it in a fictitious real-estate brochure in which our client wants only the barn and fence, not the young woman, so we need to remove her from the image. Removing her will be the easy part; rebuilding the fence will be a little tougher, but by doing it, you'll learn a valuable technique for rebuilding missing parts of an image. We'll start our project with the easiest part first by using the Rubber Stamp tool to clone grass over her legs.

STEP TWO: With the Rubber Stamp tool, hold the Option key (PC: Alt key) and click your cursor once in the grass about 1" from the young lady's legs. Move your cursor over her legs and click-and-drag to start cloning the grass. TIP: One of the secrets to making this look realistic is to avoid painting like you were painting the side of a building. If you do, you'll pick up very obvious patterns as you clone, and you'll replace her legs with an exact duplicate of the grass that you are sampling from—a dead giveaway that it's been retouched. Instead, sample once then dab the Rubber Stamp tool a few times over one part of her leg, then move to another area of grass, resample, and start again. Repeat this process of resampling and dabbing until most of her legs have been removed.

STEP THREE: Next, you're going to remove the part of the girl's head that appears between the two fence rails. There is a danger here because you might accidentally clone over one of the fence rails on either the top or bottom. There's a trick you can use that will prevent that from happening: Start by drawing a selection around the area you want to remove. This isolates that area, and you can now clone only within that selection. Try it and it'll make sense. Press Shift-L to rotate through the different Lasso tools in your Toolbox until you get the Polygonal Lasso tool (it draws straight line selections). Draw a selection between the two rails as shown here. Now you've isolated that area.

STEP FOUR: Press "s" to switch back to the Rubber Stamp tool, then Option-click (PC: Alt-click) on the woodpile that appears between the two rails. (Note: Although you can only clone inside the selected area, when choosing an area to sample from, you can click either inside or outside the selection.)

Now, move the Rubber Stamp tool over the woman's head and start painting (cloning) the woodpile until she's gone. Press Command-D (PC: Control-D) to Deselect. There may be a hard edge that appears on the right side of the area where you cloned, so you'll have to choose a smaller brush and dab a little bit over the edge to make it blend smoothly.

There's one more problem. A little bit of her head is still showing on the top fence rail. You can use the exact same technique to remove that as well: (1) Use the Polygonal Lasso tool to select the top rail, (2) sample an area of fence with the Rubber Stamp tool that's just above the top of her head, and (3) move your cursor over her head, and in a few quick dabs, the top of her head is… well, history.

STEP FIVE: It's time now for a new technique. Look at the bottom fence rail. See how some of the girl is still visible? Rather than cloning over it, here's a quick trick for getting rid of the body (that doesn't require going to a bridge in New Jersey). Use the Polygonal Lasso tool to select the top half of the fence rail (as shown here).

STEP SIX: Press the letter "v" to switch to the Move tool, then hold Shift-Option (PC: Shift-Alt) and drag your selected fence rail straight down. This makes a copy of your selection, and you can drag it down until it lines up with the bottom rail of the fence (by the way, the Option/Alt key makes the copy—adding the Shift key constrains your drag so the copy moves straight down, not side to side). The copied fence rail looks too bright and really stands out. Don't worry, you're going to fix that. For now, just position it over the bottom rail, covering a good chunk of her body.

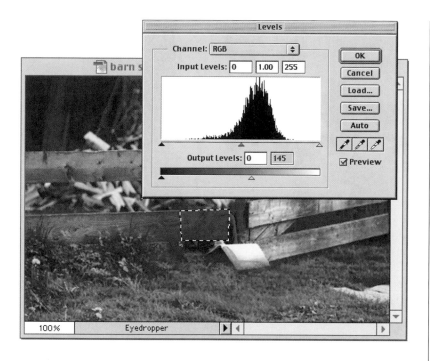

STEP SEVEN: For this next step, it helps if those pesky "marching ants" weren't encircling your selection, but we need to keep the copied fence rail selected. To hide the marching ant selection border (but to keep the selection active and in place), press Command-H (PC: Control-H) and Photoshop will hide those critters. Now, go under the Image menu, under Adjust, and choose Levels. When the Levels dialog box appears, you're going to use the Output sliders to change the tone of your copied fence rail to match the rail you copied it to. Grab the right Output Levels slider (at the bottom of the dialog box) and drag it to the left until the copied portion of the rail begins to blend in with the rest of the fence. Press Command-D (PC: Control-D) to Deselect.

STEP EIGHT: If there's an obvious edge (and there probably will be), switch back to the Rubber Stamp tool. Sample an area just to the left of the seam and dab a few times with the Rubber Stamp tool to cover it. As for the rest of the board, you don't have to make it look entirely different than the original above—just make it a bit different. In the example shown here, I only cloned over a couple of the knots in the wood along with some random dabbing. I spent all of about 30 seconds, so don't spend much more time than that. Keep in mind that it doesn't have to look completely different to be convincing. When you've cloned in the grass, press Command-D (PC: Control-D) to Deselect.

Getting rid of the rest of her body below the rail is a cinch. Use the Polygonal Lasso tool (or even the Rectangular Marquee tool) to select the area below the rail, and in about 20 seconds you can clone grass right over her, leaving just three minor items to address: (1) fixing the posts, (2) removing what's left of her between the posts, and (3) fixing the lower-right fence rail.

STEP NINE: We'll do 'em one at a time, starting with the posts. We'll use the same technique that we did for the rails. Use the Polygonal Lasso tool to select the top half of the left fence post above the top rail. Press the letter "v" to switch to the Move tool, hold Shift-Option (PC: Shift-Alt), and drag the post downward to fill in the spot where the post should appear between the top and bottom rails. You may have to drag it once, pause, release the mouse button, then click-and-drag another copy a little bit lower to fill in the area. Click-and-drag more copies to fill in the area between the bottom rail and the ground.

STEP TEN: When the last piece of post reaches the ground, deselect by pressing Command-D (PC: Control-D). Use the Rubber Stamp tool and try to find an area of grass where the blades are sticking up a bit, and clone that around the base of the post. Repeat this process for the fence post on the right side of the fence: Select a small area of the post, switch to the Move tool, hold Shift-Option (PC: Shift-Alt), and click-and-drag as many copies as you need, pausing and releasing the mouse button between each copy. Don't forget— when this copied post reaches the ground, clone in some grass near the base here, as well. Take a look at the image at right; the girl is almost gone.

STEP ELEVEN: The next step is to remove the remaining part of the girl that is still lurking between the posts—you probably already know what to do. Isolate the area with a selection, then use the Rubber Stamp tool to clone grass over that area.

STEP TWELVE: The final step is to fix the right bottom fence rail. We'll use the same technique we used on the left fence rail. First, use the Polygonal Lasso tool to select the second rail from the bottom (not the whole thing, just enough to cover the area that we need to replace on the bottom rail), then hold Shift-Option (PC: Shift-Alt) and drag yourself a copy of this rail and position it over the bottom rail. You can use Levels again to darken the selected rail just a bit by dragging the right Output Levels slider a little to the left. Lastly, use the Rubber Stamp tool to clone over a few of the knots, and add any additional grass along the bottom that's needed. As you can see, by applying this technique to the barn photo, it's as Hall and Oates once said, "She's gon-on-on-on-on-on-oh-oh-ohh… ey-e."

Removing Harsh Shadows with the Clone Stamp Tool

One casualty of digital camera use is the harsh shadows that can be produced by their flashes. In this example, we'll show a technique for dealing with those harsh shadows, and (if you should choose) replacing it with a shadow of your own.

STEP ONE: Open the image containing the harsh shadows that you want to fix (in the example shown here, the image was taken with a digital camera with a built-in flash under low lighting).

STEP TWO: You'll need to isolate the image from the background using one of Photoshop's selection tools. In this example, I was able to use the Lasso tool to make a selection around just the front of the subject (that's where the harsh shadow appears) by tracing around the edges, but you can use any tool you're comfortable with to make the selection (Pen tool, Magnetic Lasso, etc.). The back of the person didn't matter because the shadow is in front of him, so I just made a wide, loose selection behind him.

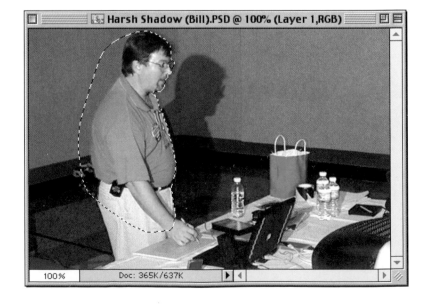

STEP THREE: Once your selection is in place, press Command-J (PC: Control-J) to put your selected object (in this case, a man) onto its own separate layer above the Background layer.

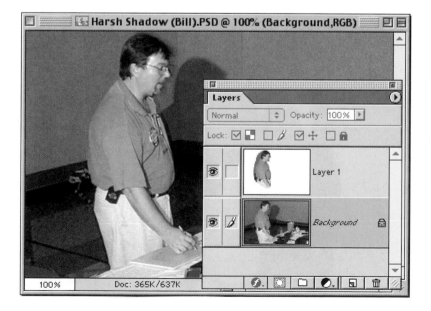

STEP FOUR: In the Layers palette, click on the Background layer to make it the active layer. Even though you'll be working on the Background layer, you can leave the object layer (Layer 1) visible. Press the letter "s" to switch to the Rubber (Clone) Stamp tool.

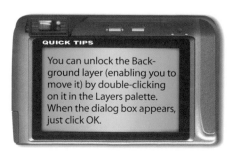

QUICK TIPS

You can unlock the Background layer (enabling you to move it) by double-clicking on it in the Layers palette. When the dialog box appears, just click OK.

STEP FIVE: The idea here is to clone over the area with the harsh shadows. Normally, this would be pretty tricky, but by putting the object onto its own layer, it's now fairly easy to clone behind it without accidentally erasing it. Here's how: First, in the Options Bar of the Rubber Stamp tool, choose a soft-edged brush from the Brushes pop-down menu. Then Option-click (PC: Alt-click) once just outside the shadow area in a portion of the background that doesn't contain any harsh shadows. Next, move your cursor over the shadow area and start clicking and dabbing over the area to clone the clean background over the harsh shadows. I started on the wall to his right, and erased some of the easy areas. Then I Option-clicked (PC: Alt-clicked) on the rug, beside the water bottle, to sample the clean area of the rug, and then painted over the shadows there. I did the same for the wood trim on the wall.

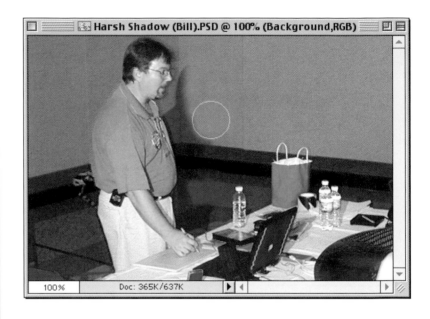

STEP SIX: As you're cloning, don't freak out if your cursor moves under your image (some people think they might damage the subject of the image, but remember, you isolated the subject on its own layer, so don't sweat it). Continue cloning until the harsh shadows have been removed. Remember, don't "whitewash the fence." Instead, click-and-dab and keep resampling from other areas right around the shadow to keep from giving away the fact that the background has been retouched. In this particular image, I had to sample from the carpet behind his (ahem) buttocks, and then move the cursor over the carpet to his right and clone that in. I did the same with the wood trim in the corner—I sampled from the wood trim behind his back.

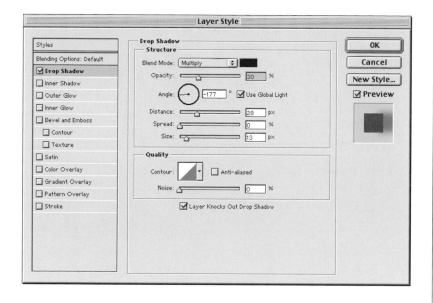

STEP SEVEN: Now you have to decide if you want to add your own shadow or leave the image as is. I say add the shadow and then decide if it looks better or not. In the Layers palette, click on the subject layer (Layer 1). At the bottom of the palette, click on the small black circle with an "*f*" in it, and a pop-up menu will appear. Choose Drop Shadow to bring up the Drop Shadow Layer Style dialog box. You'll need to do three things in this dialog: (1) increase the amount of blur (Size) to soften the shadow, (2) lower the Opacity to make it less noticeable, and (3) move your cursor outside the dialog box and click-and-drag the shadow into position. (Hint: for a realistic shadow, place it where the old shadow used to be.) Because I used a low-res digital camera image, I increased the Size (amount of blur) to 13 and lowered the Opacity to 30%. Click OK when the settings look good to you.

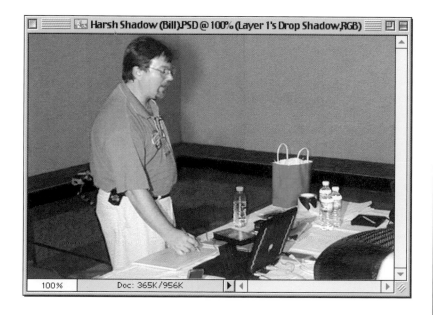

STEP EIGHT: Once you've applied the drop shadow, click the Eye icon to the left of the Drop Shadow effect to toggle the shadow on and off. You'll have to make the call whether you feel the image looks better with or without the shadow. If you decide it looks better without, click on the Drop Shadow effect and drag it into the Trash at the bottom of the Layers palette to delete the effect from your image.

Cloning from Layer to Layer or from Document to Document

There are a couple of issues you might run into when cloning, so I thought I'd take a page and address them. The first is an option's setting you can change to enable you to clone from layer to layer. The other is how to clone from document to document (betcha didn't even know you could do that).

FROM LAYER TO LAYER: By default, Photoshop allows you to clone (sample) from your current layer to another area on that same layer. What it won't let you do (by default) is sample from one layer and clone to a different layer. However, there is an option setting that will let you do this. First, choose the Rubber Stamp tool, then in the Options Bar, click on the Use All Layers checkbox. Now you can clone images from any visible layer to your active layer.

FROM DOCUMENT TO DOCUMENT: You can clone from one open document to another; the only rule to remember is both documents have to be open in Photoshop at the same time. Here's how:

STEP ONE: Open the image you want to clone from (in this case, some hundred dollar bills). Switch to the Rubber Stamp tool and Option-click (PC: Alt-click) on the area you want to clone.

STEP TWO: Open the image you want to clone into (in this case, the *Wall Street Journal* image), and start painting with the Rubber Stamp tool. You'll notice that the crosshair appears in the money image, but the paintbrush cursor appears on the newspaper image, so you can see where you're painting (cloning).

OK, in the first chapter you learned how to use the Rubber Stamp (excuse me... Clone Stamp) tool, and it

Spare Me the Details
essential retouching techniques

would make perfect sense to immediately put it to use in Chapter Two, right? Ah, but that's exactly what they'd expect me to do, wouldn't they? (By the way, who are they?) Instead, I'm going to move onto some other essential techniques that mostly rely on other parts of Photoshop, such as Layers and the History palette. This chapter should really be called "Cheating" because Photoshop does so much of the work for you that you'll feel bad about sending out an invoice for it. Not bad enough that you won't send it, but certainly bad.

It's kind of like that joke about the repairman who kicks the side of the refrigerator and the problem instantly goes away. He hands the customer a bill for $125 and the customer is furious at being charged $125 for kicking a refrigerator. He tells the customer, "I didn't charge you $125 for kicking the refrigerator. The kick was free—the $125 is for knowing where to kick." This chapter teaches you where to kick. (Hint: Aim for the compressor.)

Repairing Images that are too Light (Overexposed)

This is a trick to bring back contrast and detail in images that are overexposed. The detail is usually still there, you just have to bring it out, and this is about the quickest, easiest way to bring this type of image back to life.

STEP ONE: Open an image that is over-exposed and lacking detail.

STEP TWO: Make a copy of the image by dragging the Background layer to the New Layer icon at the bottom of the Layers palette. This will create a layer titled "Background copy."

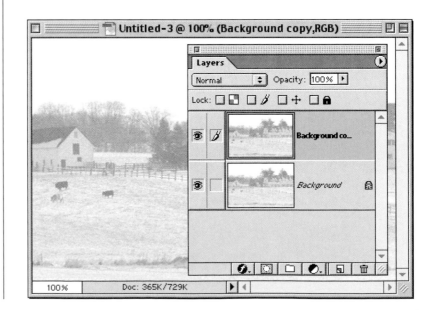

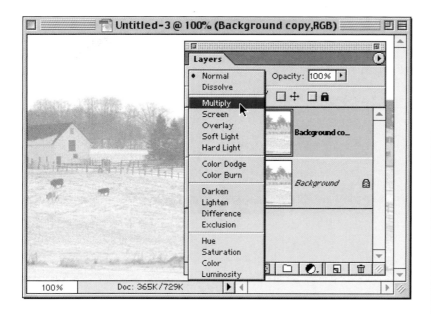

STEP THREE: Change the blend mode of the Background copy layer from Normal to Multiply in the pop-up menu at the top of the Layers palette. This will darken your image.

STEP FOUR: If the image is still overexposed, continue making copies of the top layer by dragging it to the New Layer icon until the image has sufficient detail. Sometimes you'll find that the last Multiply layer you add makes the image too dark. If so, lower the opacity of your top layer. When it looks good, you'll probably want to flatten the image, and then go into Levels/Curves to make further corrections, but this technique will quickly give you something to work with.

QUICK TIPS

To jump directly to the Multiply Blend mode for the current layer, press Shift-Option-M (PC: Shift-Alt-M).

Repairing Images that are too Dark (Underexposed)

In the previous technique, we showed you how to repair overexposed images using the Multiply mode. Now, we're going to take a look at the flip side—taking an underexposed image and lightening it using a similar trick.

STEP ONE: Open an underexposed image. This technique works for both color and grayscale images.

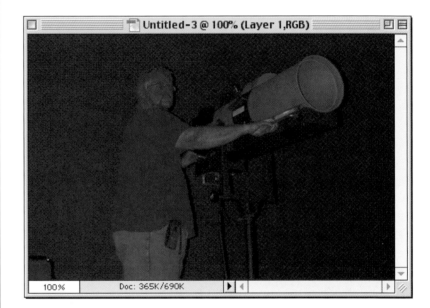

STEP TWO: In the Layers palette, drag the Background layer to the New Layer icon at the bottom to make a duplicate of the layer. On the Background copy, change the blend mode from Normal to Screen. You should see your image lighten considerably, but it may not be enough (depending on how dark the image is).

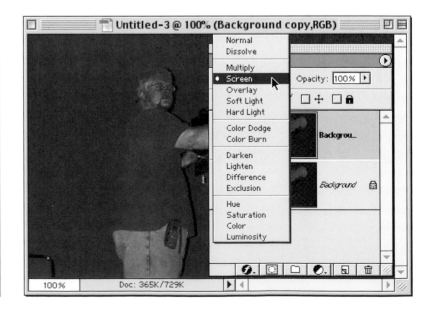

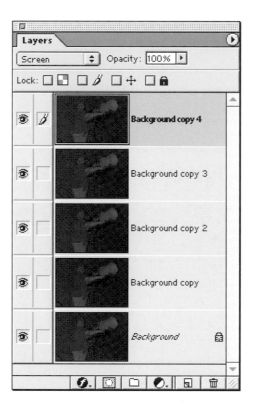

STEP THREE: If the image isn't light enough, make another copy of this duplicate layer by dragging it to the New Layer icon in the Layers palette. You can continue this process of dragging the top layer to the New Layer icon until the image looks about right (in the example shown here, it took me six copies to get the image to the point where it was light enough).

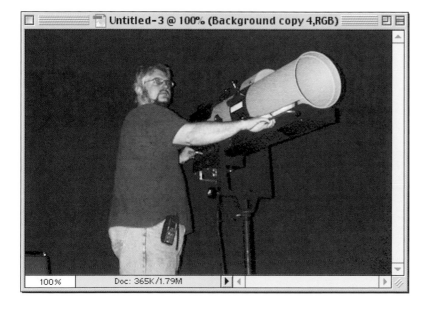

STEP FOUR: It's almost guaranteed that while performing this technique, the last Screen mode layer you add will make the image too light, but removing it makes it too dark. Here's what to do: Lower the opacity of the top layer to "dial in" the perfect blend of layers, giving you something between the full intensity of the layer, and no layer at all.

QUICK TIPS

To make a duplicate of the current layer, press Command-J (PC: Control-J).

Selectively Painting in Detail with Complete Control

The previous two tricks do a great job of bringing back overall detail and depth to overexposed/underexposed images, but they're very global changes, affecting the entire image at once with the same amount of adjustment. However, often you'll find that the whole image isn't the exact same exposure, and some areas need to be lightened and others darkened. This technique allows you to do both.

STEP ONE: Open an image that needs selective retouching for detail and contrast.

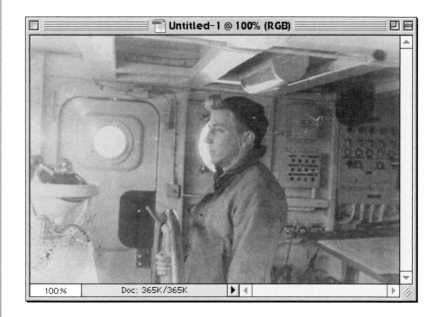

STEP TWO: Go to the pop-down menu in the Layers palette and choose New Layer. We're creating a new layer through the pop-up (rather than just clicking on the New Layer icon at the bottom of the Layers palette) because we need to access the New Layer dialog box for this technique. You don't get the dialog when you use the New Layer icon.

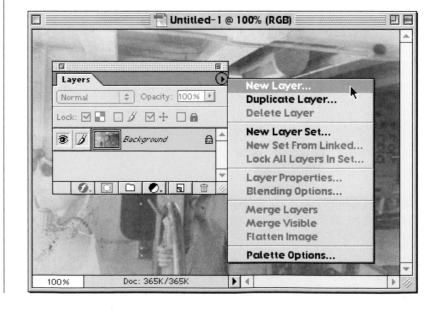

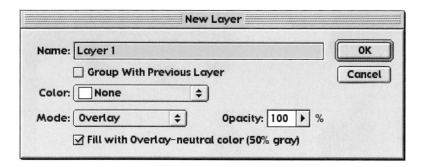

STEP THREE: In the New Layer dialog box, change the Mode from Normal to Overlay. When you do this, a new choice will appear below the Mode pop-up. It will now read "Fill with Overlay-neutral color (50% gray)." Click the checkbox to make it active, then click OK.

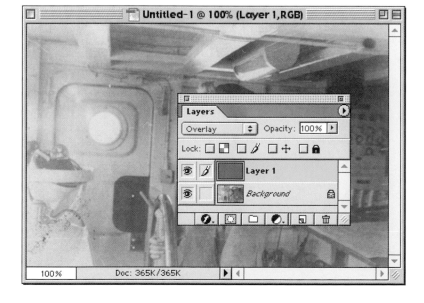

STEP FOUR: This creates a new layer above your Background layer. Although we chose to fill with 50% gray, the Overlay mode ignores the color. You'll see a gray thumbnail in your Layers palette, but the layer will appear transparent on screen.

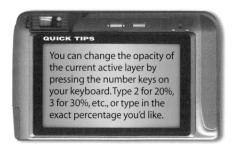

QUICK TIPS

You can change the opacity of the current active layer by pressing the number keys on your keyboard. Type 2 for 20%, 3 for 30%, etc., or type in the exact percentage you'd like.

STEP FIVE: Now comes the fun part. First, press the "d" key to reset your foreground/background colors to their default settings (black/white). Press the "b" key to switch to the Paintbrush tool. Choose a soft-edged brush from the Brushes menu in the Options Bar at the top of your screen (click on the down-facing arrow next to the brush tip thumbnail to get to the Brushes menu). Lower the opacity setting for the brush to 20%, and begin painting in your image. With black as your foreground color, the image will darken as you paint, much the same way the previous technique did, except the effect will appear only where you paint.

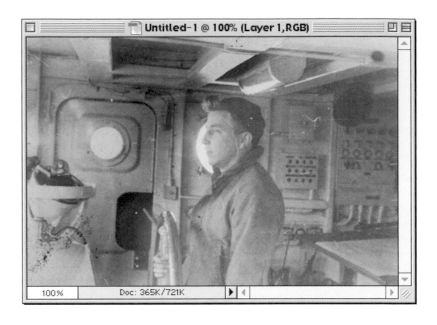

STEP SIX: Since you're painting at 20% opacity, you can always paint over the same area again to darken it. To do this, you have to release the mouse button and click again before you paint over it.

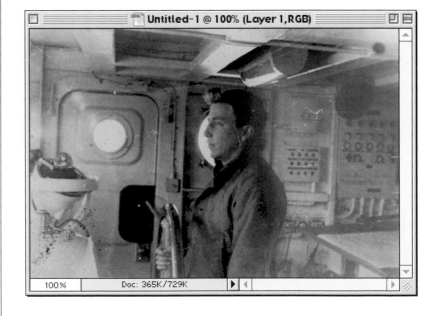

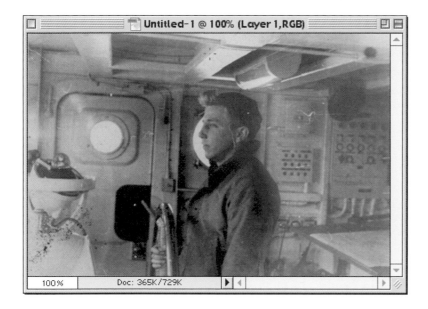

STEP SEVEN: In this particular image, you can see that the right side of the image is much darker than the left side, and our retouch has left some areas too dark. We can selectively lighten these areas by pressing the letter "x" to make the foreground color white. In the Options Bar make sure your opacity is still set to 20%, for your Paintbrush and begin painting over the areas that need to be lightened. Remember, if you paint once and it's not enough, release the mouse button, click again, and paint over the same area. You can continue switching between black and white to either darken or lighten your image as you paint.

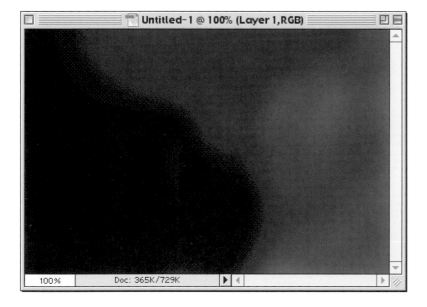

STEP EIGHT: This isn't a pretty shot (at left), but I thought you should see it anyway to help you understand what's happening in Overlay mode. If you hide your Background layer (leaving only your Overlay layer visible) this is what you'll get. You can see where you have painted and how the levels of gray affect your image. You don't need to do this step at all, I just wanted to show you what it looks like. Lovely isn't it?

Retouching Images where the Subject is in Shadows

Here's a technique using the History Brush for dealing with an image where the background looks good and well-lit, but the subject is in shadows. In the example shown here, we have an image of a building taken on a bright sunny day—the problem is that the sun is behind the building, leaving it totally in the shadows.

STEP ONE: Open an image where the subject or focus of the image appears in shadows.

STEP TWO: Go under the Image menu, under Adjust, and choose Levels. Drag the middle Input Levels slider to the left until the object in shadows looks light enough. You can do this without any regard to what's happening to the background. You can also move the far right highlight slider to the left if the midtone slider doesn't bring out the image enough—but be careful not to overdo it. As you can see, the background is getting totally blown out, but don't worry, just continue lightening the image. When your subject area looks bright enough (in this case the building), click OK.

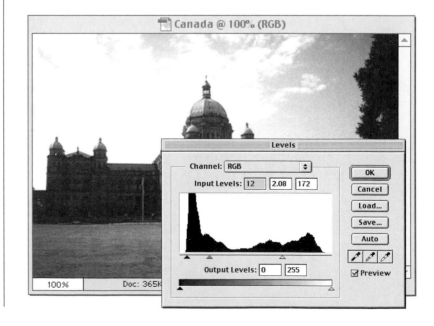

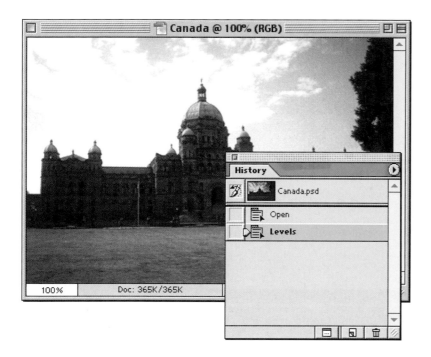

STEP THREE: Go under the Window menu and choose Show History. This gives a running "history" of the adjustments you've made to your image. In this instance, there should only be two entries (called "History States"). Open should be the first state, followed by Levels. This shows that you opened an image and then made a Levels adjustment (which is exactly what you did).

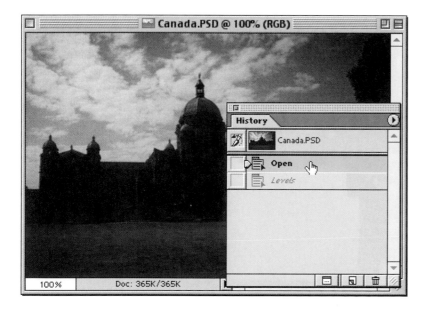

STEP FOUR: In the History palette, click on the state named "Open." On screen, this will return your image to how it looked when you originally opened the image.

QUICK TIPS

There's a keyboard shortcut for accessing multiple undo's by stepping back through History. Just press Option-Command-Z (PC: Alt-Control-Z) to move back one step at a time.

STEP FIVE: In the History palette, click in the first column next to the grayed out state named "Levels." An icon that looks like Photoshop's History Brush will appear in the column, showing that you're going to be painting from what your image looked like at that point in your correction process (which was when you lightened the image using Levels).

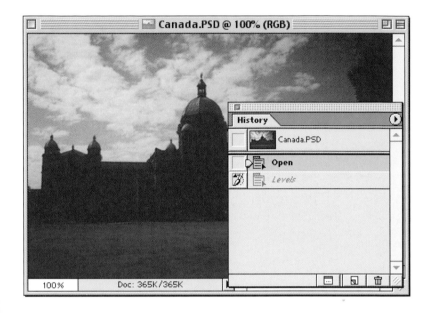

STEP SIX: Switch to the History Brush by pressing the "y" key. In the Options Bar, click on the down-facing arrow next to the brush tip thumbnail to bring up the Brushes menu. Choose a soft-edged brush from the menu.

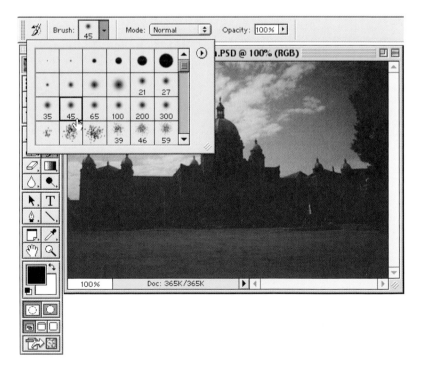

STEP SEVEN: Begin painting directly over the subject in shadows, avoiding the background area entirely. As you paint, you'll notice that you're actually painting in the lightened version of the subject you adjusted earlier with Levels.

STEP EIGHT: If your painting appears too intense, lower the opacity of the History Brush. Now when you paint, the intensity will be less. There's no need to flatten the image because you've been working on the Background layer the entire time.

Increasing Highlight (or Shadow) Detail

This is a great trick for adding detail to either the highlight or shadow areas of your image. Selecting just the highlight areas can really be a tall order, but there's actually a keyboard shortcut that will load the highlights. Once you've done that, Photoshop can do most of the work for you.

STEP ONE: Open an image that has an area lacking detail. In this example, we're using an image of a couple in the snow. The snow doesn't appear to have a lot of detail, so we'll focus on enhancing those areas.

STEP TWO: Press Option-Command-~ (PC: Alt-Control-~). Note: The ~ key is the tilde key, found just above the Tab key on your keyboard. Pressing this keyboard shortcut automatically loads a selection of all the highlights in your image, and better yet, it slightly feathers the selection so the edge transitions are soft.

STEP THREE: When the highlight selection loads, there are probably areas selected that you don't want. In the image at left, we want to bring out the detail in the snow, but as you can see, the couple is also selected. To remove them, press the "L" key to switch to the Lasso tool. In the Options Bar, in the Feather field, enter 3 (to soften the edges of the selection we're about to draw). Hold the Option key (PC: Alt key) and draw a selection around the couple. This will remove them from the current selection, leaving just the snow highlights selected.

STEP FOUR: While the selection is still in place, press Command-J (PC: Control-J) to put the highlights' selection onto its own layer. In the Layers palette, you'll now see two layers: your original Background layer and a layer that contains the highlights in your image. Before we forget, go back to the Options Bar and set the Lasso tool's Feather setting back to zero.

STEP FIVE: At the top of the Layers palette there's a pop-up menu for changing the blend mode of the currently active layer (how the layer interacts with the layers beneath it). In this pop-up menu, change the blend mode of your highlight layer (Layer 1) from Normal to Multiply. When you do this, you'll start to see a little more detail appear in the snow.

STEP SIX: Although changing the layer's blend mode to Multiply added more detail in the snow, it also darkened the trees in the background. This may seem surprising since the trees didn't appear as part of the selection, but in fact, the luminosity of the trees was selected as well, and we don't want to affect the trees—just the snow. Press the letter "e" to switch to the Eraser tool. Choose a soft-edged brush and erase over the trees. When you do this, you'll see their original brightness return. This "erasing of the Multiply layer from the trees" probably looks very subtle here in the book, but it will appear more apparent on your screen. To see the difference, press Command-Z (PC: Control-Z) a few times to get a before and after (that's the shortcut for Undo and Redo).

STEP SEVEN: To bring out even more detail in the snow, go to the Layers palette and make a duplicate of your Multiply layer (Layer 1) by clicking and dragging it to the New Layer icon at the bottom of the Layers palette. You'll really start to see the detail appear, but since we used feathered selections, the transitions appear very smooth.

STEP EIGHT: Lastly, we'll duplicate the top layer (Layer 1 copy) one more time to complete the effect. Notice how much detail has been brought out in the snow, but the rest of the image (the couple, the sled, the woods behind them) looks as it did when we first opened the image.

Note: This trick can also be used in reverse if you want to adjust just the shadows (rather than the highlights). Here's how: After you load the Luminosity, go under the Select menu and choose Inverse. This gives you the shadows instead of the highlights. The only other change is this: Once you have the image on its own layer, instead of switching the mode to Multiply, switch it to Screen. That's it!

Selective Sharpening

Later in the book, we show how to sharpen your overall image, but there are certain instances in which you may only want to sharpen one area of your image. In this example, we're going to sharpen some jewelry to make it really pop, drawing attention to just those areas.

STEP ONE: Open the image containing areas you want to sharpen (in this example, we're going to sharpen a necklace). Press Shift-R until the Sharpen tool appears in the Toolbox (it looks like a thin, white triangle). In the Options Bar, lower the pressure setting to 20% (at its default setting of 50%, you don't have enough control over the amount of sharpening—the effect seems too intense. If you want a more intense effect, you can always brush over the image area again).

STEP TWO: Before we actually use the tool, we're going to switch the image mode to Lab Color so that our sharpening doesn't interfere with the color of the image, bringing out unwanted color shifts, halos, or other nasties. Another good thing about the Lab Color mode is that it doesn't damage our image—you can move safely back and forth between RGB and Lab without worry. To make the conversion, go under the Image menu, under Mode, and choose Lab Color. Now, go to the Channels palette (under the Window menu, show Channels) and you'll see four channels. Click on the Lightness channel to make it active. This is where we'll apply our sharpening.

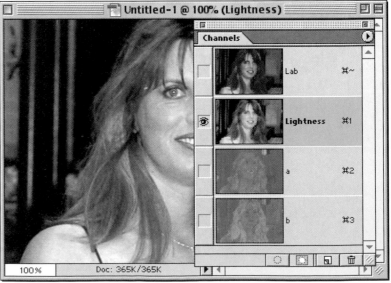

STEP THREE: When sharpening in Lab Color mode, you're only sharpening the luminosity of the image, not the color, so the Lightness channel will appear on screen in black and white—don't let that throw you. Choose a soft-edged brush that is just about the same size as the necklace (or object you want to sharpen) from the Brushes pop-down menu in the Options Bar. Then, with the Sharpen tool, paint a few strokes over her necklace. You'll immediately see them start to leap out of the image, drawing attention to the necklace. It looks brighter, sharper, and really draws your eye.

STEP FOUR: When you've sharpened all the areas you want, convert back to RGB Color by going under the Image menu, under Mode, and choosing RGB Color. Compare the image shown here in Step Four with the image shown in Step One, and you can clearly see how the increase in sharpness and clarity draws your eye to the necklace.

   This manual sharpening technique works particularly well on objects that have a metallic quality to them.

Enhancing Shadows with the Burn Tool

Sometimes you might want to add extra shadows to your image, perhaps to accentuate the drama in the image or focus attention on, or away, from an object in your image. Photoshop's Burn tool is ideal for this kind of task, and it's very easy to use, especially with the few tips we're going to give you here.

STEP ONE: Open an image that has shadows you want to accentuate. Press Shift-O until the Burn tool appears in the Toolbox (it looks like a hand forming a circle). Up in the Options Bar, lower the pressure setting to 20% and choose a medium-sized, soft-edged brush.

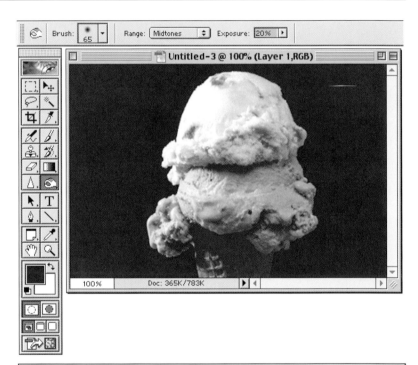

STEP TWO: Just like we did with the manual sharpening in the previous technique, we're going to first convert to the Lab Color mode to keep our burning from creating any undesirable color shifts. To make the conversion, go under the Image menu, under Mode, and choose Lab Color. Now, go to the Channels palette (under the Window menu, show Channels) and you'll see four channels. Click on the Lightness channel to make it active.

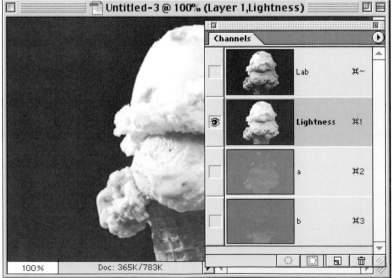

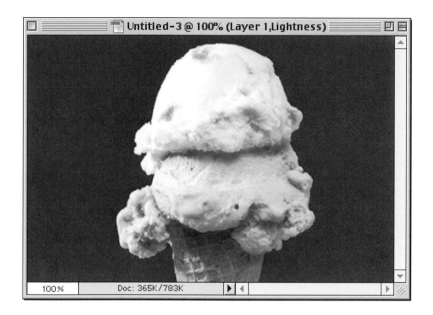

STEP THREE: Use the Burn tool to darken under the right edge of the top scoop of ice cream. Then, burn in extra shadows below the bottom scoop around the cone. To really make it look "chunky," dab a few strokes over areas where there are crevices or indentations in the image. This will give it more depth and fullness. I basically went around the image and dabbed over all those types of areas. This especially enhanced the chunks of strawberries in the top scoop, making them look richer and darker without affecting the rest of the image.

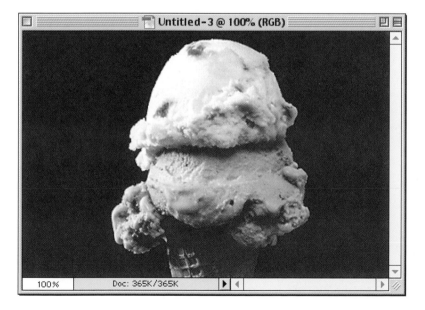

STEP FOUR: When you're finished burning the shadows you want enhanced, convert back to RGB mode by going under the Image menu, under Mode, and choosing RGB Color. I also applied an Unsharp Mask with the settings of Amount: 85, Radius: 1, Threshold: 4. Now you can see the final effect of your burning—a chunkier, yummier image with more depth and less calories.

CHAPTER THREE

I remember reading an article a couple of years ago by a retoucher who commented that, on average, it took

Face-off
digital plastic surgery

her three days to retouch a photograph in Photoshop. I thought to myself, "If she's got a client base that, on average, would pay for three days of retouching, she's my hero. I want to go to her studio and study everything she does—the way she walks, the way she answers the phone, what she has for lunch, etc.—because she has powers that should be studied on a university level." If I ever sent one of my clients a bill for three days of retouching, they'd have to use dental records to identify my body.

Maybe it's because the typical client stuff I've run into is "Can you make me look thinner, younger, smarter (always a tough one), add more hair, remove a blemish, or attach an extra set of arms protruding from my head." (OK, I only had that last one once.) In this chapter, we'll look at some quick tips that will let you send an invoice for three days' retouching that actually only took you three minutes. If your client actually pays the invoice, you're now ready to bid on big government contracts.

Removing Signs of Aging

This is a quick way to seamlessly remove wrinkles, lines, and the general effects of aging in photos of both men and women. Of the clients who've asked me to do this type of retouch, it's usually men. Well, it's certainly mostly men. OK, I admit it, it's been all men, and a female client has never asked me for this type of retouch. Will it work for women? Let's try it.

STEP ONE: Open an image of a person who needs facial retouching to eliminate signs of aging.

STEP TWO: Double-click on the Quick Mask Mode icon at the bottom of the Toolbox. This brings up the Quick Mask Options dialog. When it appears, make sure Selected Areas is the chosen option in the Color Indicates section, then click OK.

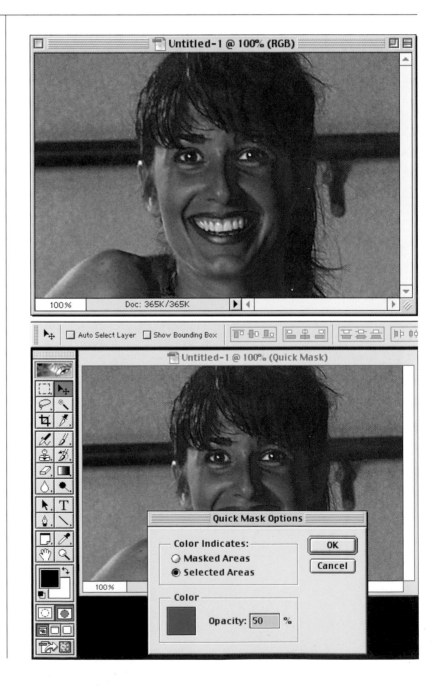

STEP THREE: Press the "b" key to switch to the Paintbrush tool. Choose a small, soft-edged brush from Brushes menu in the Options Bar and paint directly over any facial areas that show signs of aging. As you paint, your paint strokes will appear in a 50% tint of the color red. Don't worry, you're not actually painting on your image, you're painting in Quick Mask mode. The red indicates where your selected areas will be when you leave Quick Mask mode.

STEP FOUR: Make sure that you *do not* paint over any areas that have defined edges, such as the lips, edges of the face, eyebrows, eyelids, the edges of the nose, etc. If you paint over these areas, the image will look too soft and obviously retouched.

QUICK TIPS

In Quick Mask mode, if the default red mask color is hard to see, double-click on the Quick Mask icon and change the color in the Options dialog.

STEP FIVE: When you've "painted" over all the areas that need retouching, switch from Quick Mask mode back to Standard mode by pressing the "q" key or clicking on the Standard Mode icon at the bottom of the Toolbox. When you switch to Standard mode, you'll notice that the areas you painted (while in Quick Mask mode) have now become selections. (That's the beauty of Quick Mask mode: you can use the Paint tool to create selections.)

STEP SIX: While these selections are active, press Command-J (PC: Control-J) to put them onto their own layer.

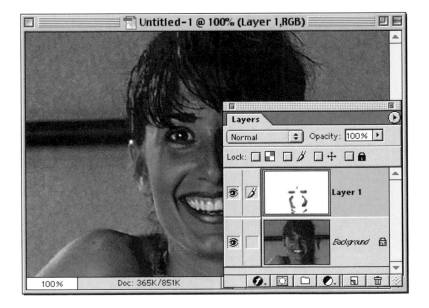

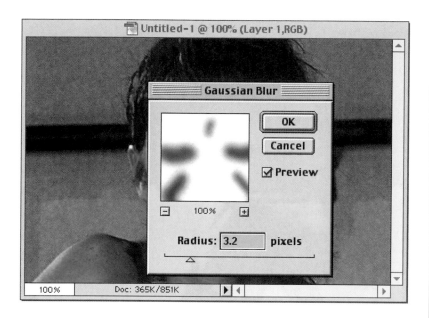

STEP SEVEN: Go under the Filter menu, under Blur, and choose Gaussian Blur. Start with a 4-pixel blur (try 8 for high-res, 300-ppi images) and the wrinkles should disappear. You can increase/decrease the amount of blur until it looks smooth. As long as the preview checkbox is turned on in the Gaussian Blur dialog box, you can simply move the slider to see the results live on screen.

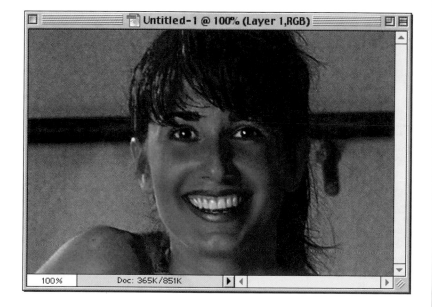

STEP EIGHT: You can decrease the intensity of the softening effect by lowering the Opacity slider on your layer. The lower the opacity, the more of the original image (or aging) will show through. Complete the retouch by going to the pop-down menu in the Layers palette and choosing Flatten Image. If the image lost too much of its sharpness, go under the Filter menu, under Sharpen, and choose Unsharp Mask. Try applying an Unsharp Mask with these settings: Amount: 100, Radius: 1, Threshold: 5. This should bring back some of the sharpness to the image.

Wrinkle Removing (Method Two)

I would recommend using this wrinkle-removing technique on images where you need to keep the maximum amount of detail. The previous technique had you blurring part of the skin to smooth wrinkles, and although that technique may work fine in many instances, sometimes it removes too much detail. When you have an image with crisp details, try this technique instead, created by Adobe's graphics evangelist (and Photoshop madman) Russell Preston Brown.

STEP ONE: Open a detailed image with a headshot that needs wrinkles removed.

STEP TWO: Press the letter "s" to bring up the Rubber (Clone) Stamp tool. In the Options Bar, choose a soft-edged brush that's approximately the size of the wrinkles you want to eliminate. The key to this technique is changing the tool's Blend Mode from Normal to Lighten and then lowering the tool's Opacity to 50%. This enables you to adjust only the dark areas of the face, affecting as few pixels as possible and leaving the detail in areas that don't need adjusting.

STEP THREE: Take the Rubber Stamp tool and Option-click (PC: Alt-click) right beside one of the wrinkles to sample that area. Then move your cursor over the wrinkle and paint right over the wrinkle (you may have to paint a few strokes over the same area to remove the wrinkles). By using Lighten mode, you're only painting away the wrinkles, without affecting the other pixels in those skin areas that contain details you want to keep. In the example shown here, I painted around the man's eyes (to remove the crow's feet), and between his eyes on the bridge of his nose. You can see what a dramatic effect this has already had. You shouldn't need to spend much more than 20–35 seconds retouching these areas—just a few brush strokes over each wrinkle will do the job.

STEP FOUR: Continue this technique of sampling near the wrinkles then cloning over them with the Rubber Stamp tool set to Lighten. In the example shown here, I moved down from the eye area to the smile lines on his face. I also retouched his upper lip, some other areas around his lips, and anywhere I saw a telltale wrinkle. The total retouch should take you about two minutes. Compare the image here in Step Four, with the image we started with in Step One.

QUICK TIPS

Once you have a paint tool, including the Rubber Stamp tool, you can toggle through the tool's blend modes by pressing Shift-+.

Brightening Teeth

This is a simple technique, but it can be surprisingly effective. Because Photoshop has so many tonal adjustment tools, there are a number of different techniques you could use for brightening the teeth. In this case, we're going to use a simple adjustment that anyone can do, regardless of their Photoshop experience.

STEP ONE: Open an image of a person whose smile you want to enhance by whitening his/her teeth. In the image shown here, the young man has dull, yellowish teeth.

STEP TWO: Press the "L" key to switch to the Lasso tool. Using the Lasso, draw a selection around the teeth you want to whiten. Then, go under the Select menu and choose Feather. When the Feather dialog box appears, enter a Feather Radius of 1 and click OK (for high-res, 300-ppi images, enter a Radius of 3).

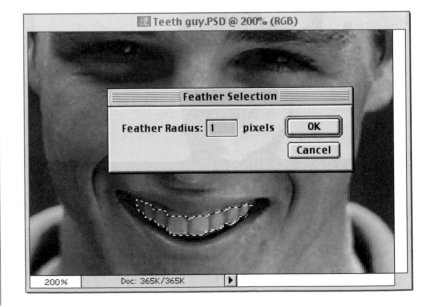

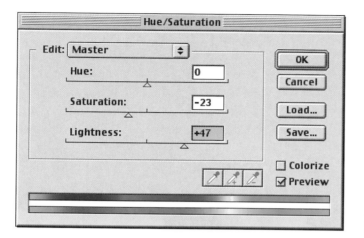

STEP THREE: Go under the Image menu, under Adjust, and choose Hue/Saturation. When the dialog box appears, move the Lightness slider (the bottom of the three) to the right to brighten the teeth. Be careful not to over-brighten or it will draw too much attention to the teeth, and they'll look obviously retouched. Also, if the teeth start to look like they're glowing, lower the amount of saturation by dragging the Saturation slider to the left.

STEP FOUR: When the amount of brightness looks right, click OK. Lastly, deselect the teeth by pressing Command-D (PC: Control-D).

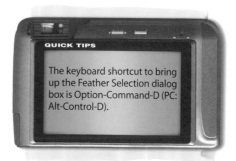

QUICK TIPS

The keyboard shortcut to bring up the Feather Selection dialog box is Option-Command-D (PC: Alt-Control-D).

Removing Red Eye

Now that everybody and his brother has a digital camera, everybody and his brother has a preponderance of digital snapshots where 79.8% of the people in their photos appear to be demonically possessed. The sad part is, studies show that only 3.6% of the people in these photos are actually demonically possessed, and the rest are just the result of the flash being mounted on the camera. Here's how to remove the red eye and, better yet, recolor the eyes in question.

STEP ONE: Open an image that contains red eye.

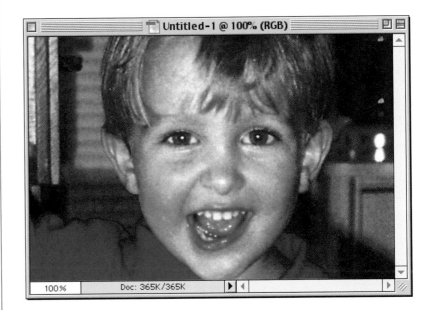

STEP TWO: Zoom in on one of the eyes using the Zoom tool. You'll have to zoom in quite a bit (perhaps as much as 1200%) to get the eye big enough to make the adjustment. That's one big eye. Eerie, isn't it?

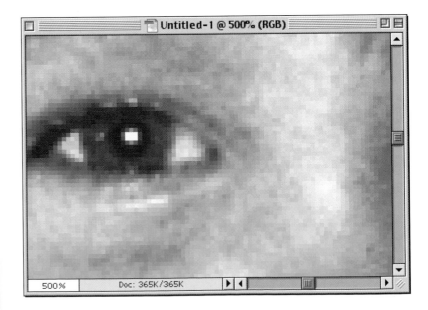

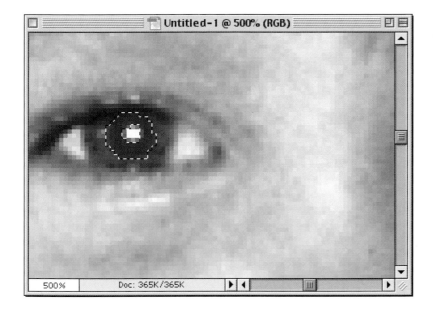

STEP THREE: Press the "w" key to switch to the Magic Wand tool, and click it in one part of the red area. In most cases, just one click will select all of the red in the eye (it's usually just one shade, so the Magic Wand works fairly well in this instance). If it doesn't select enough of the red area, hold the Shift key and click the Magic Wand again in another area of red (holding the Shift key lets you add to your current selection). If it selects too much, go up to the Options Bar, lower the Threshold number and try again. You may have to lower it to less than 10 to get just the red areas selected. Once one eye is selected, scroll over to the other eye, hold the Shift key, and select it the same way so that both eyes are selected.

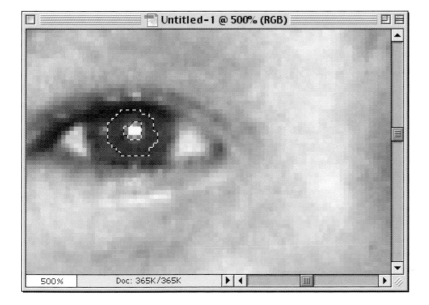

STEP FOUR: Once you have the red areas well selected (you don't have to have every single pixel, just get pretty close) press Shift-Command-U (PC: Shift-Control-U) to remove all the color from the red areas of the eye. This is the shortcut for Photoshop's Desaturate command. This leaves the eye looking gray, so we have to touch it up a bit.

QUICK TIPS

You can zoom out when using the Zoom tool by holding the Option key (PC: Alt key) and clicking within your image.

STEP FIVE: Press the "d" key to set your foreground color to black. Press the "j" key to switch to the Airbrush tool. Go up to the Options Bar and lower the Opacity setting to 20%. In the Options bar, next to the brush-tip thumbnail, click the down-facing triangle to make the brushes menu visible. Choose a medium to large-sized, soft-edged brush.

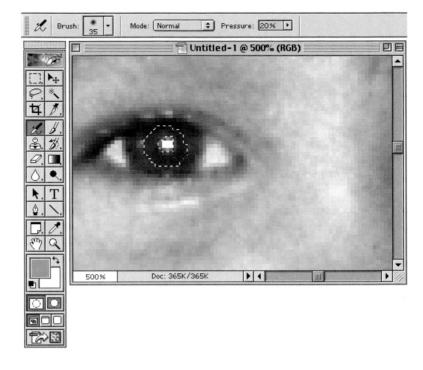

STEP SIX: Zoom out by pressing Command-–(the minus sign) (PC: Control-–) until you can see both eyes on screen. Paint just a couple of strokes over the selected areas of the eye. This won't turn the eye completely black, but it will make it a very dark gray. Don't overdo it, just a couple of strokes will do.

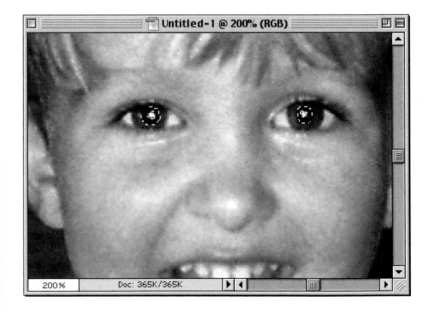

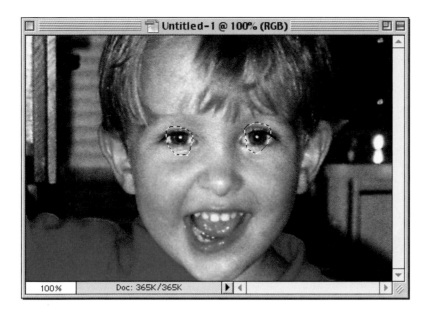

STEP SEVEN: Deselect the eye by pressing Command-D (PC: Control-D). Press the "L" key to switch to the Lasso tool. Now, drag a loose selection around the entire cornea of the eye. It does *not* have to be a precise selection, just a loose selection is fine, as long as the whole area is enclosed within the selection.

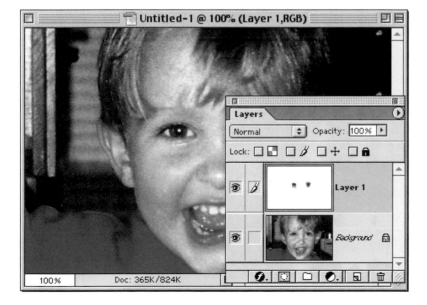

STEP EIGHT: Now, press Command-J (PC: Control-J) to put the eye selection on its own layer.

STEP NINE: Go under the Image menu, under Adjust, and choose Hue/Saturation. In the dialog box, click on the Colorize checkbox (found in the bottom right-hand corner). Now you can choose the color you'd like for the eye by moving the Hue slider. The area you removed earlier will remain the dark gray color, and only the cornea will be affected by your colorization. In this case, we're going to colorize the eye blue. Here's a hint: Choose a shade that's actually lighter than you think it should be, and perhaps lower the amount of Saturation (using the slider), or the eyes will look artificially enhanced.

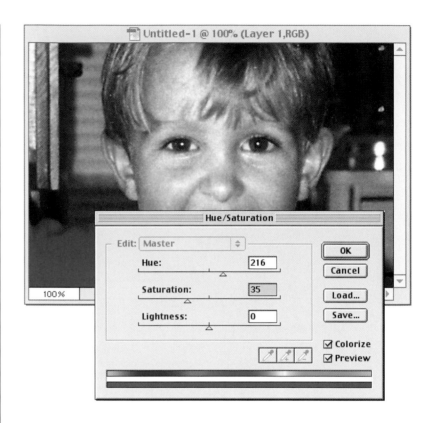

STEP TEN: Press the "e" key to switch to the Eraser tool, and then erase the extra areas around the cornea from your loose selection. This sounds much harder than it is—it's actually deceivingly easy—just erase everything but the blue cornea. Don't forget to erase over the whites of the person's eyes. Remember, the eyes are on their own layer, so you can't accidentally damage any other parts of the image.

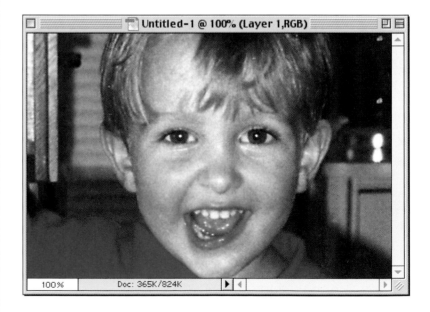

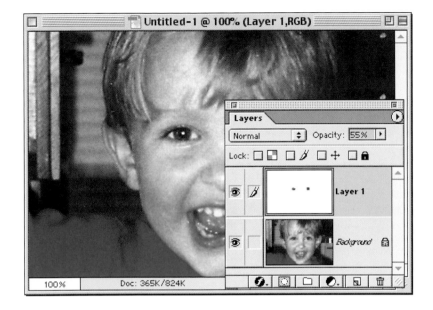

STEP ELEVEN: It seems there's a tendency to add too much color to the eyes, but luckily, you can control the intensity after the fact. Just go to the Layers palette and lower the opacity of your eye layer. As you lower the opacity, the intensity of the color will subside. Keep lowering it until you find a more realistic-looking color.

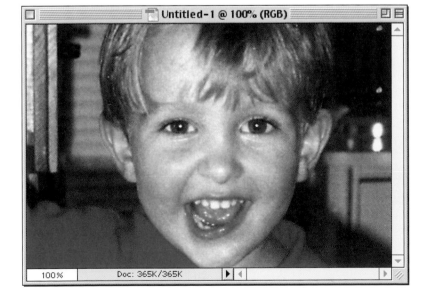

STEP TWELVE: To finish up, press Command-E (PC: Control-E) to merge the eye layer with the Background layer, completing the retouch.

Red-eye Removal Quick Tip

On the previous pages, we showed a detailed step-by-step process for not only removing red eye but also for recoloring the eye itself. But sometimes you don't need that level of detail—you just want the red eye gone, you don't care to recolor the eye, and you only want to spend 10 seconds on it. If that's the case, try this!

STEP ONE: Open the image that contains red eye. Press the letter "b" to switch to the Paintbrush tool. In the Options Bar, change the tool's blend mode from Normal to Color. Also, choose a soft-edged brush that's just about the size of the red eye itself.

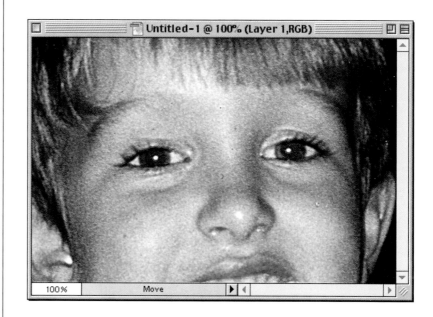

STEP TWO: Use the Paintbrush tool to quickly paint directly over the red eye. As you paint, the red eye disappears instantly. Why? Because when you set the Paintbrush tool to Color mode, basically, it's just desaturating (removing the color from) the places you paint. It's quick, it's easy, and it takes less than 10 seconds.

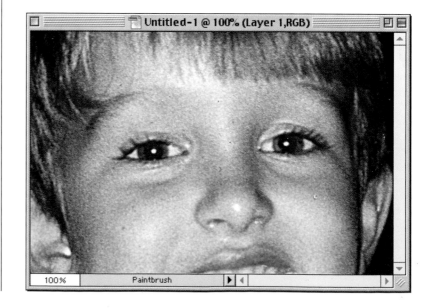

Nose Reduction

There's just no pretty way to say, "make my nose smaller," so the best I could come up with is the official sounding "nose reduction" and, basically, that's what we'll do with this simple facial retouching technique.

STEP ONE: Open the image that needs an application of the "schnozalator."

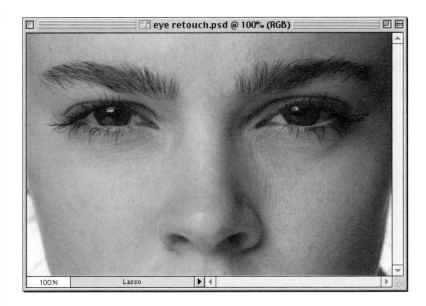

STEP TWO: Press the "L" key to switch to the Lasso tool, and draw a loose selection around the nose. Make sure you don't make this selection too close, or too precise—you need to capture some flesh tone area around the nose as well (as shown here).

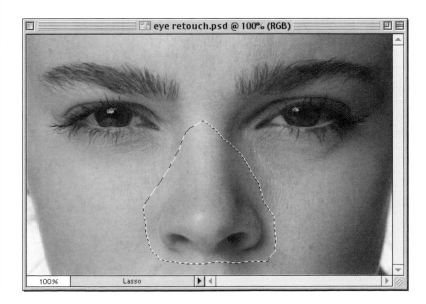

STEP THREE: To soften the edges of your selection, go under the Select menu and choose Feather. When the Feather Selection dialog box appears, for Feather Radius enter 4 pixels (for high-res, 300-ppi images, enter 8 pixels) then click OK.

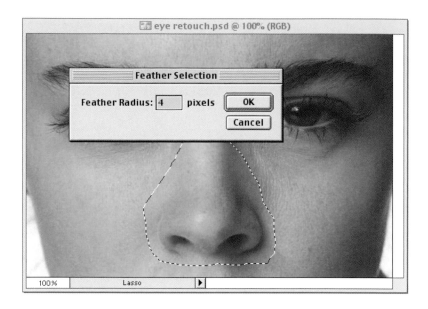

STEP FOUR: Now, press Command-J (PC: Control-J) to put your selected area onto its own layer in the Layers palette.

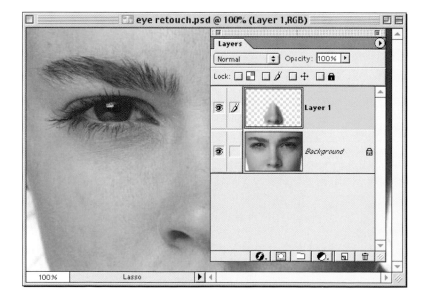

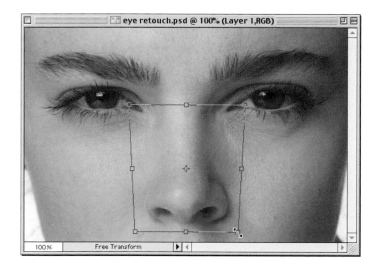

STEP FIVE: Press Command-T (PC: Control-T) to bring up the Free Transform bounding box. Control-click within the bounding box (PC: Right-click) and a pop-up menu of possible transformations will appear. Choose Perspective from the list. Then grab the bottom right-hand corner transform point and drag inward to shrink the bottom of the nose, while leaving the top of the nose (nearest the eyes) pretty much untouched.

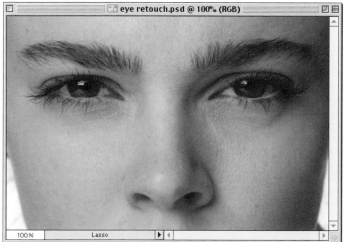

Before

STEP SIX: When the new size looks about right, press Return (PC: Enter) to lock in your changes. If any of the old nose peeks out from behind your new nose, then click on the Background layer and use the Rubber Stamp tool to clone away those areas: Sample an area next to the nose, and then paint (clone) right over it. Compare the before shot (top left) versus the retouched version (bottom left) and you can see what a dramatic change our 30-second retouch had on the image.

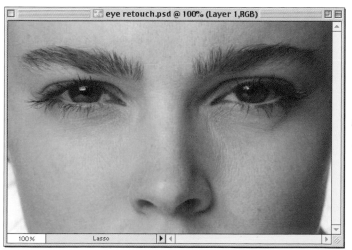

After

Enhancing Eyes

When you're retouching a portrait, arguably there's nothing more important than how the eyes look. This technique is a quick and easy way to enhance the eyes by removing undesirable elements and adding brightness and clarity, which can make a world of difference.

STEP ONE: Open the image that needs eye enhancement.

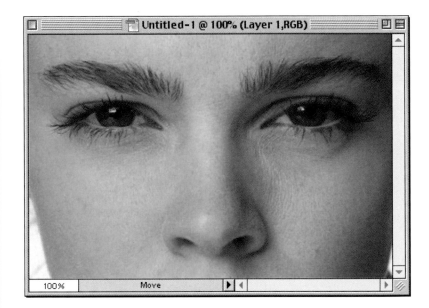

STEP TWO: Press the "L" key to switch to the Lasso tool, and make a selection around one of the white areas of one of the eyes (you may have to zoom in a bit to make an accurate selection). Hold the Shift key and draw selections around all of the other white areas of both eyes to add them to your selection. Once you have all of the white areas of the eyes selected, go under the Select menu and choose Feather (to soften the edges of your selection). When the dialog box appears, enter a Feather Radius of 1 pixel and click OK. (Note: for high-res, 300-ppi images, try 3 pixels.)

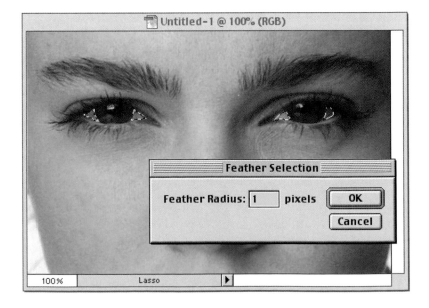

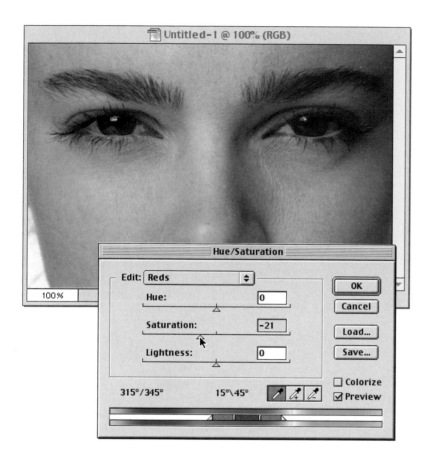

STEP THREE: We need to keep the feathered selection active, but it will be helpful to hide the selection border (the "marching ants") from view, so press Command-H (PC: Control-H) to hide it. Now you can see your retouch without being distracted. Go under the Image menu, under Adjust, and choose Hue/Saturation. The first thing we need to do is remove some of the red that appears in the white areas of the eye (a little bit of red, or a tiny bit of bloodshot eye is fairly common). When the dialog box appears, from the Edit pop-up menu at the top, choose Reds. To reduce the reds in the eye, reduce the amount of saturation by sliding the Saturation slider to the left until the red is gone. Don't click OK quite yet.

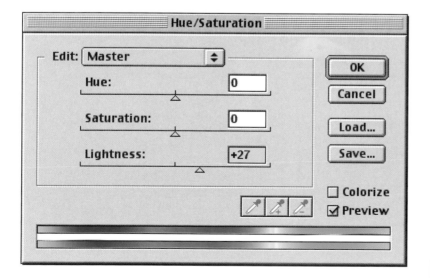

STEP FOUR: From the Edit pop-up menu in the Hue/Saturation dialog box, return the menu to Master. Now you're going to increase the brightness of the whites of the eyes by moving the Lightness slider to the right. Make sure the Preview checkbox is turned on, and look at your image as you drag—you'll see the eyes begin to brighten. Don't overdo it or it will look unnatural. You only need to slide it enough to have nice bright, clear eyes.

STEP FIVE: When you click OK, the eyes should look much better—any redness should be gone, and the whites of the eyes should be a brighter white. Now, even though you can't see it, the whites of the eyes are still selected. Remember, we just hid the selection from view. So press Command-H (PC: Control-H) to view the selected areas again, then press Command-D (PC: Control-D) to Deselect.

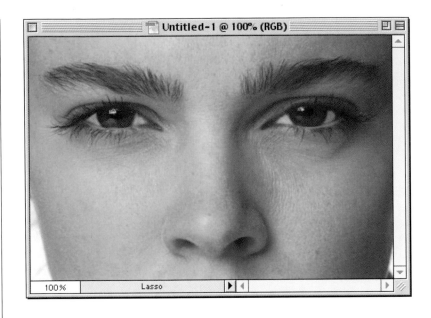

STEP SIX: Next, we'll bring some sparkle and sharpness to the eyes by sharpening them. Go under the Filter menu, under Sharpen, and choose Unsharp Mask. When the dialog box appears, enter Amount: 65, Radius: 4, Threshold: 3, and then click OK. Press Command-F (PC: Control-F) to run the filter again using the same settings. Although the eyes should really "pop" now, the rest of the face will be drastically oversharpened, perhaps to the point that it looks damaged.

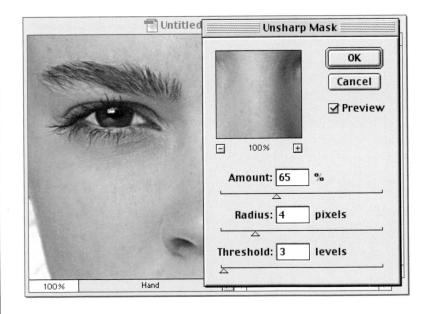

QUICK TIPS

If you wind up using the same Unsharp Mask settings often, you can create an Action for each of them, and assign them to F-keys on your keyboard.

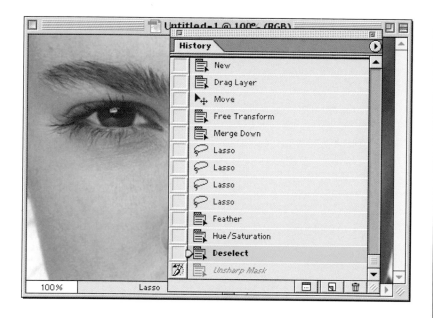

STEP SEVEN: Go under the Window menu and choose Show History. In the History palette, the last "state" in the list should be Unsharp Mask. Directly before Unsharp Mask should be Deselect. Click on the Deselect state. This returns your image to how it looked immediately before you applied the Unsharp Mask. Now, click your cursor in the first column next to the grayed-out Unsharp Mask state (don't jump to that state, just click in the first column to the left of it. A History Brush icon will appear there). You're telling Photoshop you want the ability to paint from how the image looked after you ran the Unsharp mask filter.

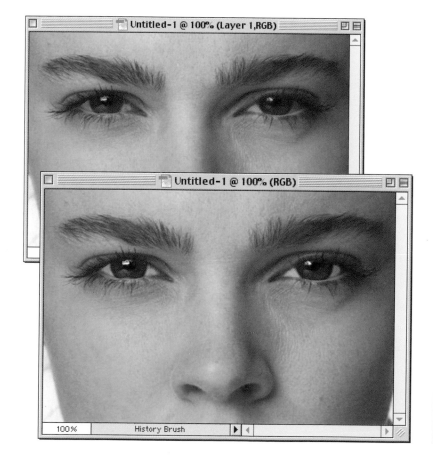

STEP EIGHT: Press the letter "y" to switch to the History Brush. Choose a soft-edged brush that is approximately the size of the cornea of the eye and paint (dab) directly over that area of the eye. As you paint, the sharpened eye will paint in (remember, you're painting from how the image looked after you applied the Unsharp Mask). The eye should now have a crisp sharpness, while the rest of the face remains untouched. You can see the before and after shots at left (the before is at the back, and the after is in front).

Removing Braces, Shadows, and Other Blemishes

This is more like a project, than just a single technique, because it uses some of the skills you've already learned in previous techniques here in the book and applies them to a real-world example. In the image we use here, we want to remove the braces, brighten the teeth, remove a blemish on the nose, remove the shadows under the eyes, and sharpen.

STEP ONE: Open the image that needs facial retouching. In this case, we're going to start by removing the braces.

STEP TWO: To work on the braces, you're going to have to zoom in a bit, so press the "z" key to switch to the Zoom tool, and drag out a rectangle around the lips and mouth to zoom in on that area (when zooming in, the image may look pixelated if it's a low-resolution image taken with a digital camera, as this one is).

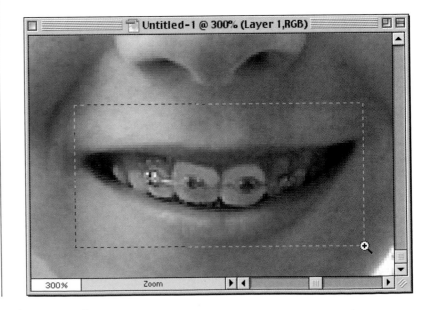

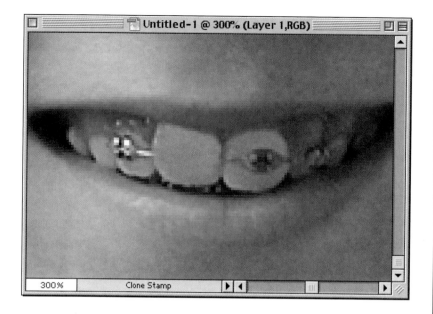

STEP THREE: The technique here is the same technique you learned in Chapter One using the Rubber (Clone) Stamp tool. Choose a very small, soft-edged brush from the Brushes menu in the Options Bar. Hold Option (PC: Alt) and click on the tooth just above the braces to sample from that area. Now, move over the braces and click-and-dab to clone over them. Once you've removed the top portion of the braces, you can increase the size of your brush, because now there's more room to sample from a clean area. Don't forget to resample in clean areas of the tooth fairly often, and don't sample too far away from where you're cloning or you'll pick up tonal changes that will be a dead giveaway that it's been retouched.

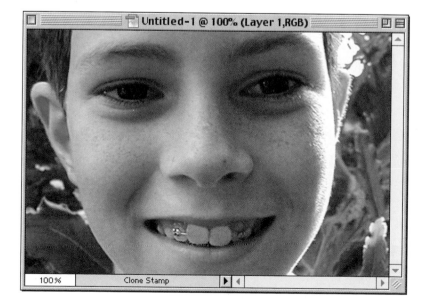

STEP FOUR: After the front tooth is done, move to the tooth to its left and repeat the same process: Sample on the tooth above the braces, then move down and clone over the braces by dabbing and re-sampling often. The key technique here is patience. Just keep sampling and dabbing, and within a couple of minutes, this tooth will be braceless, as well.

STEP FIVE: For the smaller teeth to either side, you'll probably have to zoom in even closer, but you'll use the exact same technique of sampling above the teeth and then moving down and cloning over them. Continue this process until the braces are no longer visible.

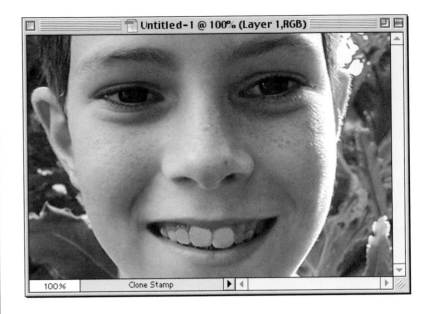

STEP SIX: While we have the Rubber Stamp tool, we may as well get rid of that blemish on the right side of his nose, near his nostril. Sample just to the left of the blemish in an area that has about the same tone as the area surrounding the blemish, then, with a soft-edged brush that's just a tiny bit bigger than the blemish itself, paint one or two little dabs and the blemish will disappear.

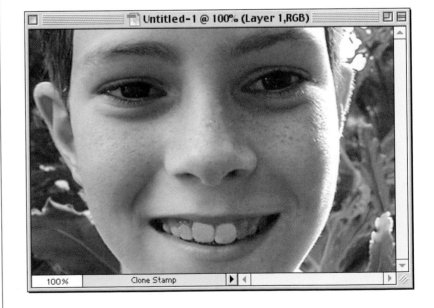

QUICK TIPS

To quickly zoom in on your image "think plus and minus." To zoom in, press Command-+ (PC: Control-+). To zoom out, press Command- – (PC: Control- –).

STEP SEVEN: Next, we're going to get rid of those shadows under his eyes. You should still have the Rubber Stamp tool selected, so go up in the Options Bar and change the blend Mode to Lighten, then lower the Opacity to about 35%. Choose a 65-pixel (or larger), soft-edged brush. Sample just below his eye in an area not affected by shadow, then paint a few strokes just under his eye in the shadows to "paint away" the shadow. Because the Rubber Stamp tool is set to Lighten, this only affects the pixels that are darker, and leaves the lighter pixels untouched, which leaves the detail intact. Pretty slick!

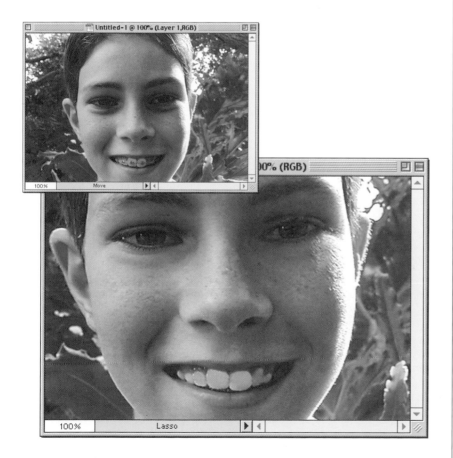

STEP EIGHT: Now for the finishing touches: To brighten his teeth, you're going to use the exact same technique as shown earlier in this chapter. You select the teeth, feather by 1 pixel, then use the Lightness slider in the Hue/Saturation dialog to brighten the selected teeth. Lastly, to increase the overall sharpness of the image, go under the Filter menu, under Sharpen, and choose Unsharp Mask. For Amount enter 85, Radius enter 1, and Threshold enter 4, then click OK to apply the overall sharpening. (Note: there's much more on advanced sharpening techniques in the "True Colors" chapter.)

Both the before (smaller inset) and the after image (larger image) are shown here. Notice how the shadows from under the eyes are gone, the braces are gone, and the teeth are much brighter? Also, the blemish from the nose is gone and the overall sharpness is increased.

Enlarging and Shrinking Facial Features with Liquify

Photoshop 6.0 introduced the Liquify feature, and many people I've talked to have dismissed it as a silly "caricature-maker," along the lines of Kai's Super Goo. But there's really a surprising amount of retouching power under the Liquify hood. Here, we're using it to enlarge and shrink facial features.

STEP ONE: Open the image that needs facial retouching. In this example, we're going to use Liquify for two tasks—enlarging the eyes to make them stand out more and, while we're at it, tweaking the nose down just a tiny bit.

STEP TWO: Go under the Image menu and choose Liquify from the bottom of the menu. This will open your image in the Liquify dialog box with its own set of tools running down the left-hand side of the dialog box. Click on the fifth tool from the top—the Bloat tool (shortcut: press the "b" key). Choose a brush that's larger than the iris of the eye, center the brush over the iris, then click two or three times over the left iris to enlarge it (don't paint or drag, just click). Do the same for the right eye—remember to use the same number of clicks for the right eye that you did for the left so the changes are uniform.

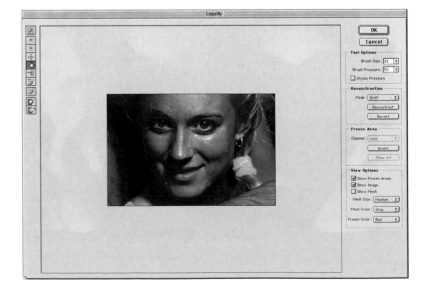

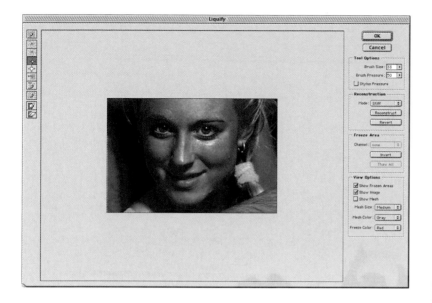

STEP THREE: Now that the eyes are enlarged, we can adjust the nose inward a little bit, so choose the tool that's just above your current tool. That's the Pucker tool (shortcut: press the "p" key). With the same brush size, dab a few times on both sides of the nose, just above the nostril, to shrink it in size. Again, remember to use the same number of clicks on both sides so it looks uniform. Also, remember not to paint with this tool (for this technique)—just click and it'll do its thing.

STEP FOUR: When the adjustments look about right, click OK. The final image is shown here. (Compare it to the image in Step One and you can see that the eyes are bigger and the nose is slightly smaller.) The best way to see the difference is to apply the changes using Liquify, then undo and redo the changes by pressing Command-Z (PC: Control-Z) a few times. You'll immediately see the difference between the two images.

CHAPTER FOUR

There must have been a point in American history where the prevailing wisdom was to store your most

Damaged Goods
repairing damaged images

precious photographs at the bottom of a bin that was also used for storing spare automobile parts. Apparently, ripping the corners and sides of photographs must have also been a popular pastime, only surpassed by the art of scotch-taping pictures back together without any regard for how they were reconnected. Seriously, what was going on back then? I wonder if anyone's ever commissioned a study to determine if there was a nationwide shortage of photo albums or other clean, dry, non-traumatic storage devices. Or was there another reason? Perhaps a communist plot that caused otherwise smart individuals to abuse their photographs in this fashion. This whole thing could be somehow tied to Stonehenge, but I can't prove it. Yet luckily, this chapter looks at the untold damage created by our ancestors and how to correct it in Photoshop.

Quick Fix for Removing Spots

Here's a technique for removing artifacts. Artifacts is a fancy "schmancy" name for spots, dust, specks, and other junk that wind up on your images—sometimes during the scanning stage, sometimes during the "toss these photos in a shoebox for 30 years" stage. The reason they're called artifacts is so that you can charge more for getting rid of them. For example, if you told a client "I've got to fix those specks on your photo," really how much could you charge? But "removing artifacts," that's a term that's worthy to appear on an invoice.

STEP ONE: Open an image that contains spots or specks in the background. Press the "L" key to switch to the Lasso tool and draw a selection around one of the areas that contains specks. This technique is ideal for situations where you don't have a detailed background (such as sky, trees, a gray studio backdrop, etc.). In the image shown here, I zoomed in on an area packed with little spots against a bland sky.

STEP TWO: Go under the Select menu and choose Feather. In the Feather Selection dialog box, choose 4 pixels for Feather Radius and click OK. Press Command-J (PC: Control-J) to put your selected area onto its own layer.

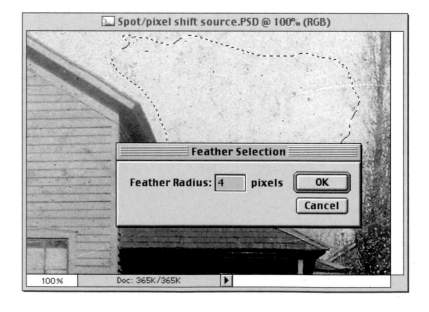

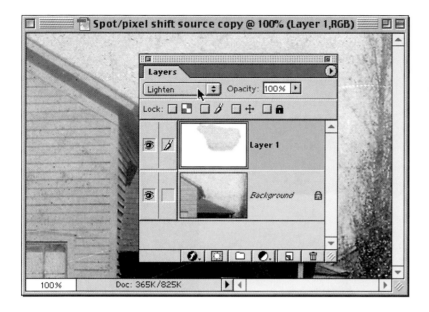

STEP THREE: Press the "v" key to switch to the Move tool. Press the Right Arrow key once and the Down Arrow key once to offset your layer down and to the right by 1 pixel from the original layer below it. In the Layers palette, change the layer blend mode from Normal to Lighten.

STEP FOUR: Continue this procedure of selecting an area with specks (from the Background layer), feathering the selection, putting it on its own layer, offsetting the new layer down and to the right by 1 pixel, and then changing the layer blend mode to Lighten until all the specks have been hidden.

QUICK TIPS

To make sure you're seeing all the specks and spots in an image, view it at 100% by double-clicking on the Zoom tool.

Tricks for Removing Moiré Patterns

Moiré pattern is a technical name for a pattern of dots, circles, or spots that appear in your image. There are a half-dozen reasons a moiré pattern might appear, but one of the most common occurs when you scan in an image that has already been printed (in a magazine, newspaper, book, etc.). What happens is the scanner picks up and magnifies or enhances the dots that were applied to the image to make it printable, creating a horrible-looking pattern that generally ruins your image. Here are four way to get rid of moiré:

MOIRÉ-REMOVAL TECHNIQUE #1

STEP ONE: Open an image that contains a moiré pattern.

STEP TWO: Go under the Filter menu, under Noise, and choose Despeckle. There's no dialog box or settings to choose, so just select the filter and it does its thing.

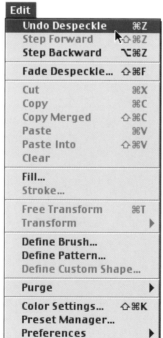

STEP THREE: When you apply the Despeckle filter, the moiré pattern should disappear.

STEP FOUR: If the moiré pattern is still visible after applying the Despeckle filter, it's important to undo the filter by going under the Edit menu and choosing Undo Despeckle. Then, try the technique shown on the next page. The reason you should undo Despeckle (if it doesn't work) is that Despeckle adds a slight bit of blur to your image. This blur is acceptable if it removes the moiré pattern, but if it doesn't work, there's no sense leaving the blur on the image. Now, on to the next technique.

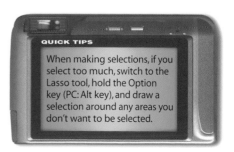

QUICK TIPS

When making selections, if you select too much, switch to the Lasso tool, hold the Option key (PC: Alt key), and draw a selection around any areas you don't want to be selected.

MOIRÉ-REMOVAL TECHNIQUE #2

STEP ONE: Here's another image that contains a moiré pattern. I tried applying the Despeckle filter to remove it, but it didn't work, so I chose Undo from the Edit menu. Now it's time to try a different moiré pattern-removal technique.

STEP TWO: Go under the Filter menu, under Blur, and choose Gaussian Blur. When the Gaussian Blur dialog box appears, enter a value of 1.

STEP THREE: The goal is to remove the moiré pattern using the smallest amount of Gaussian Blur possible. Highlight the Radius field, then press the Down Arrow key once. When you press it, the amount of blur will be lowered to 0.9 pixels. Keep pressing until you see the moiré pattern reappear, then press the Up Arrow key once to make it disappear again. I haven't been able to get away with less than 0.4 pixels in my experience, but if you can get away with it, more power to ya.

STEP FOUR: When you click OK, the pattern should have disappeared. The operative term here is "should have disappeared." If it didn't, you should employ the same tactic we did on the first technique—undo it. Then, turn the page to learn another moiré-removal trick.

MOIRÉ-REMOVAL TECHNIQUE #3
STEP ONE: If the first two techniques didn't work, try this: Go under the Filter menu, under Noise, and choose Median.

STEP TWO: A Radius of 1 pixel will normally do the trick, so enter 1 and click OK. If it works, you're set, if not, undo and move on to Technique #4.

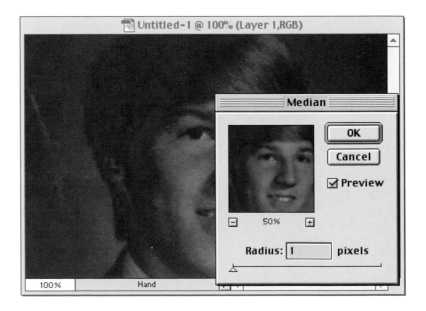

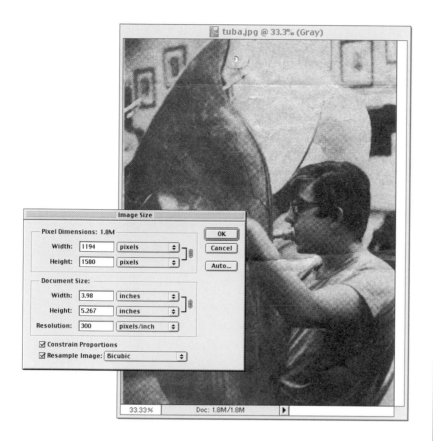

MOIRÉ-REMOVAL TECHNIQUE #4

STEP ONE: If everything else fails, lowering the resolution of your image will usually do the trick. For example, if you scanned the image at 300 dpi, you can safely lower the resolution to double the line screen of the printer you're going to output to. If it's a laser printer or color inkjet, you can safely lower the resolution to 200 ppi (which is really more than you need). In this example shown here, I started with a 300-ppi scan.

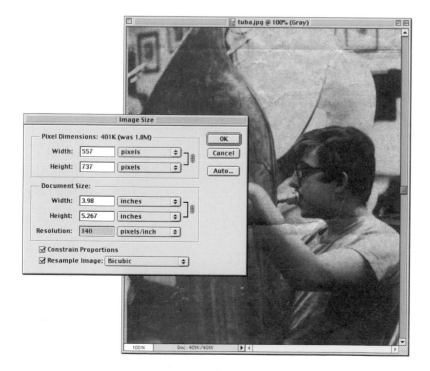

STEP TWO: Go under the Image menu, and choose Image Size. In the Resolution field, enter 140 ppi. Also, make sure the Resample Image checkbox is turned on (at the bottom of the dialog box), then click OK. As you can see, it removed the moiré pattern the other methods didn't.

If the three previous techniques didn't work, it's time to pull out the big guns. Rescan the image, *but* before you do, open the scanner lid and physically tilt your image a little to the left or right, and rescan the image. Once you've rescanned it, you'll have to straighten it using one of the techniques shown in the "Cropping and Straightening Images" chapter. Incidentally, if scanning the image at an angle doesn't remove the moiré, in many cases, the act of straightening the crooked scan will fix the moiré.

Retouching Using Define Pattern

This is a great trick for repairing damaged parts of your image with a repeating pattern, such as walls, carpeting, wallpaper, etc. Here's a step-by-step:

STEP ONE: Open an image that has a background area that needs a retouch. In this example, we've got wallpaper with plenty of damage.

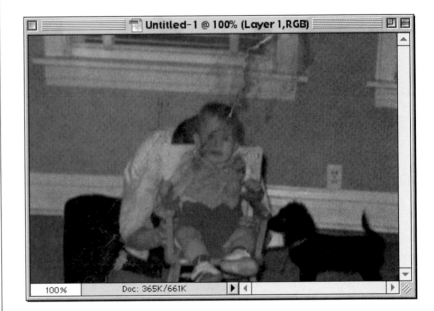

STEP TWO: Press the "m" key to switch to the Rectangular Marquee tool. Find a clean area of the background (in this case, a clean area of the wallpaper), hold the Shift key, and draw a small square selection in that clean area.

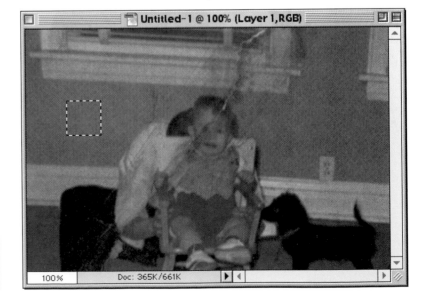

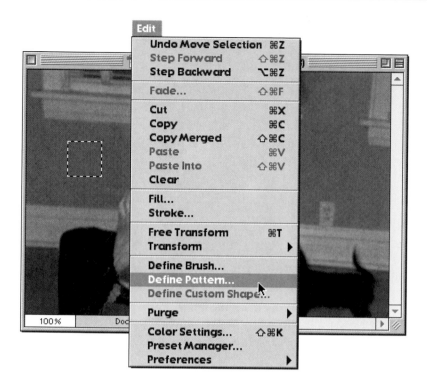

STEP THREE: Go under the Edit menu and choose Define Pattern. When the Pattern Name dialog box appears (this dialog first appeared in Photoshop 6.0), give your pattern a name and click OK. This adds the pattern to your Pattern Presets. Deselect by pressing Command-D (PC: Control-D).

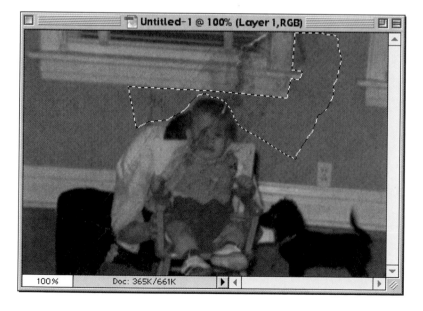

STEP FOUR: Use the selection tool of your choice (Lasso, Magic Wand, etc.) and select the area you want to retouch.

QUICK TIPS

Once you've saved a pattern, you can add it to other objects on a layer by choosing Pattern Overlay from the Layer Styles pop-up menu at the bottom of the Layers palette.

STEP FIVE: Go under the Edit menu and choose Fill. In the Contents section of the Fill dialog box, choose Pattern from the Use pop-up. The pattern you saved in the last step will now appear in the tiny thumbnail, just below the Use pop-up menu. To reveal more patterns, click the down-facing triangle to the right of the thumbnail. Make sure your desired pattern is chosen, then click OK.

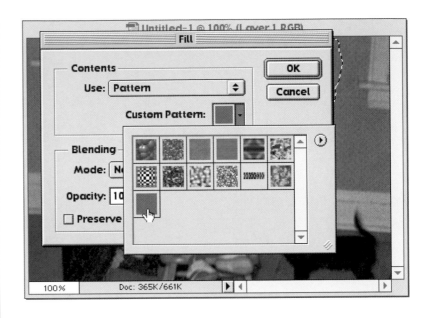

STEP SIX: When you click OK, it fills your selected area with a repeating pattern of the clean selection of wallpaper, completing the retouch .

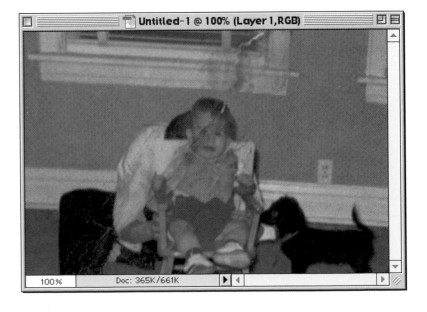

QUICK TIPS

You can bring up the Fill dialog box by pressing Shift-Delete (PC: Shift-Backspace).

Tear Fix with a Tonal Adjustment

Anytime we have a damaged area (a window, a wall, a hand, etc.), we always look for another copy within the same image that we can duplicate and flip to use for the repair. The problem is that sometimes these pasted areas don't match the same tone as the area it's pasted into. In this instance, a part of the aisle on the bottom left was torn away, so we'll copy the right side of the aisle and make a tonal adjustment for this retouch.

STEP ONE: Find a clean area of your image that you could use to cover over the damaged area. Make a rectangular selection around this area.

STEP TWO: Now, press Command-J (PC: Control-J) to put the selected area onto its own layer.

STEP THREE: You may need to horizontally flip this area so it looks realistic in your image. If that's the case, press Command-T (PC: Control-T) to bring up Free Transform. Hold the Control key (PC: Right-click) and click within the Free Transform bounding box. When the pop-up menu appears, choose Flip Horizontal.

STEP FOUR: Click inside the bounding box and drag this flipped copy into position over the damaged area, then press Return (PC: Enter) to lock in your transformation. Once you've done this, your flipped layer will probably look either too light or too dark to match the areas it's covering. In the next step, we'll adjust this retouch to match the overall tone of the underlying area.

QUICK TIPS

When using Free Transform, you can also lock in your transformation by double-clicking within the Free Transform bounding box.

STEP FIVE: Go to the Levels dialog box, make sure the Preview box is checked, and move the Output Levels slider to the right. This lightens the overall tone of the layer and you can usually create a pretty decent match within just a few seconds.

STEP SIX: In this instance, I had a little overlap that stuck into the aisle, so I switched to the Eraser tool and just… well, erased it (after all, it was on its own layer, so why not?). When the overall tone of the flipped retouch layer matches your Background layer, press Command-E (PC: Control-E) to merge these two layers together, completing this retouch.

Removing Scratches the Easy Way

This is one of my favorite retouching tricks for removing spots, scratches, dust, and other nasties (called "artifacts") from your images. I first learned this technique back when I was using Photoshop 4.0, but here, we're updating the technique, which is made easier by using Photoshop's History feature.

STEP ONE: Open an image that contains scratches, dust, spots, or other artifacts you want to remove.

STEP TWO: Go under the Filter menu, under Noise, and choose Dust & Scratches. When the dialog box appears, drag the sliders for both Radius and Threshold to the far left (Radius: 1, Threshold: 0). Then, slowly drag them to the right until the spots disappear. The image will become very blurry and appear totally unusable at this stage, but don't let that deter you. Keep dragging until the spots and other artifacts are no longer visible, no matter how blurry the image appears on screen, then click OK.

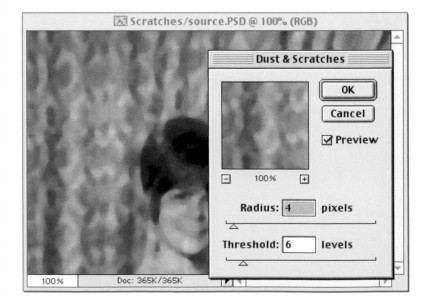

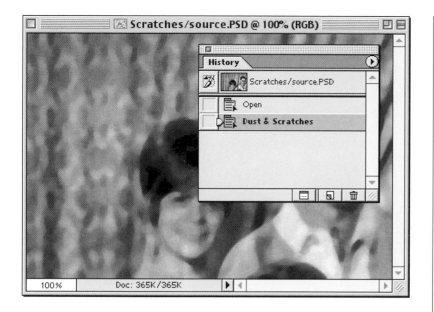

STEP THREE: Go under the Window menu and choose Show History. By default, the History palette keeps track of Photoshop's last 20 steps (called History States), but up to this point you've only performed two steps: (1) you opened the image, and (2) you applied the Dust & Scratches filter. In the History palette, click on the Open state to jump back to what your image looked like when you first opened it.

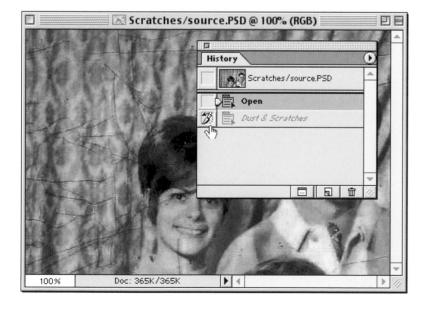

STEP FOUR: In the History palette, click in the first column beside the state named Dust & Scratches (even though it's grayed out). A History Brush icon will appear in this column. This tells Photoshop that you want to "paint" from what the image looked like after you added the Dust & Scratches filter. However, if you start painting at this point, it would simply paint in the blurry mess we created when we applied the Dust & Scratches filter, so we need to make an adjustment to the History Brush tool before we start painting.

QUICK TIPS

Another way to use the Dust & Scratches filter for removing spots is to zoom in on the spot, use the Lasso tool to make a loose selection around the spot, and then apply the filter.

STEP FIVE: Press the "y" key to switch to the History Brush tool. To get rid of dark spots within your image, change the Blend Mode in the Options Bar from Normal to Lighten (as shown here). Then, choose a soft-edged brush that's approximately the size of the spots you want to remove.

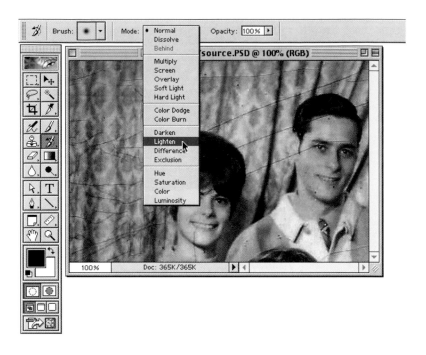

STEP SIX: Paint directly over the spots and they will disappear. Remember not to use too large a brush—choose a brush size that is very close to the size of the spots you want to remove. You may have to change brush sizes more than once to eliminate different spots or artifacts.

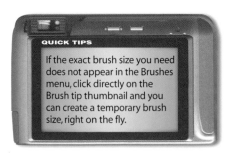

QUICK TIPS

If the exact brush size you need does not appear in the Brushes menu, click directly on the Brush tip thumbnail and you can create a temporary brush size, right on the fly.

STEP SEVEN: To remove scratches or spots that are of a lighter nature, you'll need to switch the Blend Mode (in the Options Bar) from Lighten to Darken (as shown).

STEP EIGHT: Lastly, to remove those lighter problem areas, just paint with the History Brush over those areas until they're no longer visible. In the example shown here, there were only three tiny little white dots on the man's face, so I dabbed over them and they disappeared.

Removing Spots with the Blur Tool

Here is another quick little trick for removing spots, blemishes, and other little irritating artifacts that may turn up in your images.

STEP ONE: Open the image that contains spots or blemishes.

STEP TWO: Press Shift-R until the Blur tool appears in the Toolbox (it looks like a little white teardrop).

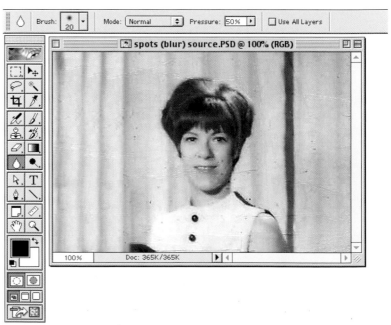

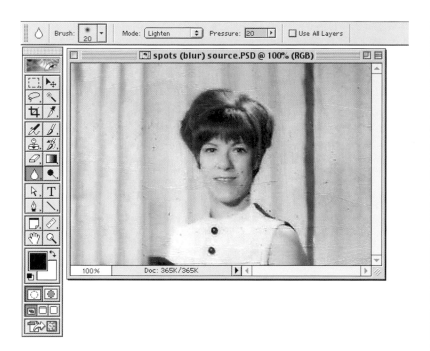

STEP THREE: Go to the Options Bar and change the painting Blend Mode to Lighten, and then lower the Opacity to 20%.

STEP FOUR: Choose a small, soft-edged brush that is approximately the width of the spot you want to repair and begin painting back and forth over the scratch with the Blur tool. You may have to make a few passes over the scratch to make it disappear. If the scratch or spot you want repaired is light in color, switch your paint blend mode to Darken, then paint over the light areas. Switch back and forth between Lighten and Darken to remove all the spots, as shown here.

Repairing Damaged Facial Features

I've always joked that anytime you have an image of a person with only one damaged feature (such as an eye, ear, arm, leg, nostril, etc.) you've got a retoucher's dream job. That's because you can usually use the undamaged eye, ear, arm, etc. to replace the damaged part. Here, we're going to copy, flip, and tweak the good eye to cover over a closed eye.

STEP ONE: Open the image that contains a damaged facial feature (in this case, it's a closed eye from a photo taken just after midnight on New Year's Eve).

STEP TWO: Use one of Photoshop's selection tools to select the good body part. In this example, I used the Lasso tool to make a selection around the eye. I was able to use a very loose selection, but depending on the image, you may have to be more precise than this. Especially if you're selecting a body part like a hand or arm.

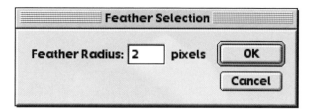

STEP THREE: To keep from having a hard edge around the selected area, you'll usually want to add a slight feather at this point. Go under the Select menu and choose Feather. When the dialog box appears, you'll need to enter a Feather Radius. For low-res images use a 1- or 2-pixel radius. For high-res, 300-ppi images you can use as much as 4 or 5.

STEP FOUR: Now, press Command-J (PC: Control-J) to put the selected area onto its own layer.

QUICK TIPS

To bring up (or hide) the Layers palette, just press F7.

STEP FIVE: We've selected the eye and put it on its own layer. Unfortunately, you can't just drag this eye over the closed eye (ahh, if it were only that easy) because you'd wind up with two left eyes, and it would look very unnatural (at best). The eye is on its own layer, so drag the opened eye layer over the closed eye. Next, you'll have to flip the eye, so press Command-T (PC: Control-T) to bring up the Free Transform bounding box.

STEP SIX: Hold the Control key (PC: Right-click) then click-and-hold inside the Free Transform bounding box. A pop-up menu of transformations will appear, and from this menu, choose Flip Horizontal.

QUICK TIPS

When using Free Transform, you can access the Distort function by holding the Command key (PC: Control key) then grabbing a corner point and dragging.

STEP SEVEN: Flipping the eye isn't going to be enough to complete this retouch—you're also going to have to rotate the eye into position. Move your cursor outside the Free Transform bounding box and you'll notice that it has changed into a two-headed arrow. Click-and-drag to rotate the eye into position. HINT: If you want to perfectly position the eye, before you perform Steps Six and Seven, lower the opacity of the eye layer to about 50%. That way you can see the closed eye below, and you can position the eye.

STEP EIGHT: When the eye is properly positioned, press Return (PC: Enter) to lock in the changes. Now you can press Command-E (PC: Control-E) to merge this eye layer with your original image below it.

STEP NINE: Since the average person's eyes generally look about the same, you shouldn't have much retouching left. One thing you can do quite easily to make the new eye look more natural is to switch to the History Brush and paint around the eye. As you brush, it will paint back the original eye, so stop just short of touching the new eye itself. This will bring back the natural look of the skin surrounding the eye.

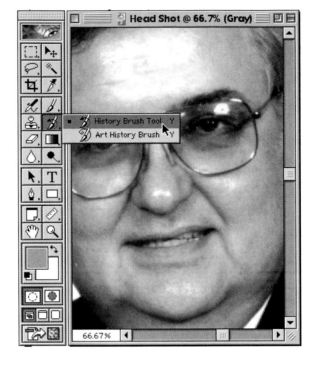

STEP TEN: At this point, you only need to retouch enough to make this eye look slightly different than the original left eye. Using the History Brush helps, but you can also switch to the Rubber Stamp tool to do some cloning around the eye—just enough to make it look slightly different. It only needs a slight retouch, so don't overdo it. If you need to, you can zoom in tight (using the Zoom tool) to complete the retouch with a tiny, soft-edged brush.

QUICK TIPS

Photoshop won't let you use the History Brush to return to previous steps once you change the color mode or resolution of an image.

CHAPTER FIVE

Originally, I wasn't going to include a chapter on getting correct color, but when I was putting this book together,

True Colors
getting your color on track

I spent so much time removing color casts, balancing colors, and doing basic color-correction tasks that without it, the book would be, well… missing an important chapter on correcting color.

Now, as I'm sure you're aware, there are entire books written on the subject of color correction. Reading one, or even all of them, won't make you a color expert. Correcting color is more of a trade, something that is learned by years of hands-on experience, trial and error, reading and learning, Cagney & Lacey, Nip and Tuck, etc. It's not something you can master just by reading a chapter in a book. So, are you doomed to having color images that look awful? Yup. Sorry. (You know I'm kidding, right?) Granted, this chapter won't make you a color-correction expert, but here's what it will do—it'll make most every color image you have look better, have more detail, look sharper, plus you'll get whiter whites and brighter brights with every wash.

Removing Color Casts

Almost every digital camera or scanner introduces some sort of color cast to every image it captures, so one of the first things you'll have to do (if you want your image to look good) is to remove those color casts. Here's a simple, step-by-step method for quickly and easily removing color casts, to give you crisp natural-looking color throughout your image.

STEP ONE: Open the RGB image that has a color cast you want to remove (again, this can be from a digital camera, scanner, photo CD, etc.). This image is of the Florida-based band Panic (some old friends of mine). From left to right that's Gary, Scotty, and Chuck.

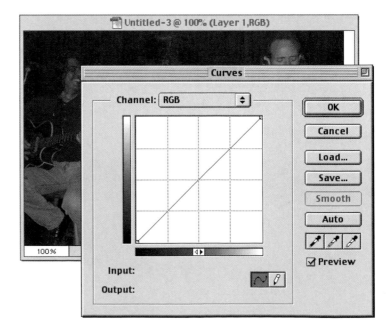

STEP TWO: Go under the Image menu, under Adjust, and choose Curves (don't worry, even if you've never used Curves before, this technique is a breeze, because we're going to let Photoshop do most of the work by making use of the Eyedropper tools located within the Curves dialog).

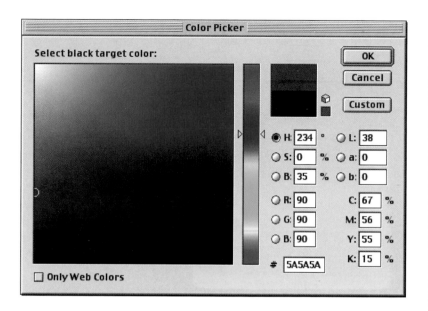

STEP THREE: Double-click on the shadow (black point) Eyedropper tool (it's the first one from the left). A dialog box will appear that looks like the standard Color Picker; however, it's not—this is a special Color Picker that resides strictly within the Curves and Levels dialog boxes. You'll notice that if you look at the top left, it's asking you to "Select black target color." This is where we'll enter values that, when applied, will help remove any color cast from the shadow areas of your image.

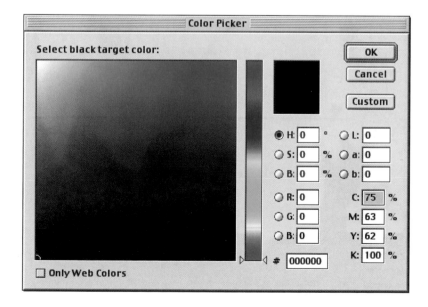

STEP FOUR: Even though we're in RGB mode, for this correction method we're going to enter CMYK values. Press the Tab key to move through the fields until you reach the field named "C" (cyan). Enter 75, then press the Tab key again to jump to the "M" (magenta) field and enter 63. Press Tab again and enter 62 for yellow ("Y"). Press Tab once more for black (the letter K) and enter either 100 (if you're going to the Web, multimedia, or creating a screen-based presentation) or 90 (if you're going to print). Click OK to lock in these values. (Note: These aren't random numbers you're entering; these are widely used to produce a neutral shadow, and they are shadow values that most printing presses can replicate without a problem.)

STEP FIVE: Now, double-click on the highlight Eyedropper (the far right of the three Eyedroppers in the Curves dialog) to bring up the white point Color Picker. For cyan, enter 5. Press the Tab key to jump to the magenta field and enter 3. Press Tab again and enter 3 for yellow . Press Tab once more for black (the letter K) and enter 0. Again, these are white point values that are widely used to produce a neutral white point without color casts that can be reproduced by most printing presses. Click OK in the Curves dialog to lock in these settings.

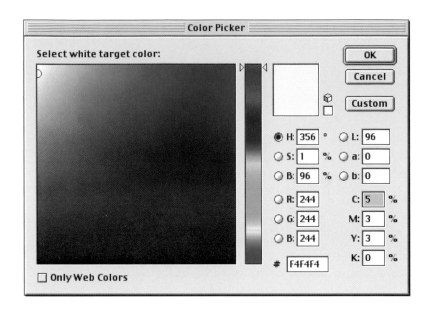

STEP SIX: At this point, the first thing to do is to determine (visually) what's the most important part of the image, meaning what is the focal point of your image. For example, if you have a couple sitting on the grass, do you want the couple to look good or the grass to look good? Unless you're doing an ad for lawn treatment, chances are you want the people to look good, so you would correct the photo to make them look their best. If the grass isn't perfect, we don't care, but the people have to be right on the money, so when we're correcting, focus on them. In this image, it's important that the musicians look good, so we'll try and focus on them or the equipment they're using. Now on to the tricky part. It's not hard; it's just a little tricky. But I'll show you a great trick to make it less tricky. (I'm not sure that makes any sense at all, but bear with me.)

STEP SEVEN: The tricky part is determining which part of the image should be the color black. Ideally, every image would have something that's supposed to be black, but of course, that doesn't always happen in real life. In the absence of something that's supposed to be black, choose the part of the image that is the darkest. Now, the darkest part of the image might be a shadowy blade of grass, so generally, we'll shoot for the darkest part of the people (since they are the focus) in the photo instead of the dark area of the grass. If they don't have a dark area, then you'll have to go for the grass, but they'll probably have some area of darkness, often in their hair, shoes, or clothing. In this case, it appears his guitar should be black, but I'm just guessing. So that's the tricky part—finding the "black point." Here's the cool trick for finding it if you're not quite sure where it is.

STEP EIGHT: Go to the Layers palette and click on the half white/half black circle icon to bring up the Adjustment Layer pop-up menu (it's the fourth icon from the left). When the menu appears, choose Threshold. (I'm not going to explain the whole Adjustment Layer thing here; understanding it won't matter for this technique, so keep rolling ahead.) When you do this, a new layer will be added to your Layers palette. If you expand your Layers palette far enough out to the right, you'll see the word "Threshold" on this new layer. If not, you can see it's a different kind of layer, because instead of a thumbnail picture, there's an icon that looks like a square with a little slider underneath it. This is to let you know that this is not a standard layer but an editable Adjustment Layer. (See the Layers palette shown in the next step.)

STEP NINE: When the Threshold dialog box appears, your image will turn into a black-and-white bitmapped image (don't worry, press on!). Drag the Threshold Level slider under the Histogram (which looks like a mountain range) all the way to the left. Your screen will turn entirely white. Slowly drag the Threshold slider back to the right, and as you do, you'll start to see some of your bitmapped image reappear. The first things that appear are the darkest parts of your image. There, you just tricked Photoshop into telling you exactly where the darkest part of the image is. In this instance, a lot of his guitar appears to be the darkest part of the image so that's my target. Make a mental note of where the darkest part is, and click OK to close the Threshold dialog box.

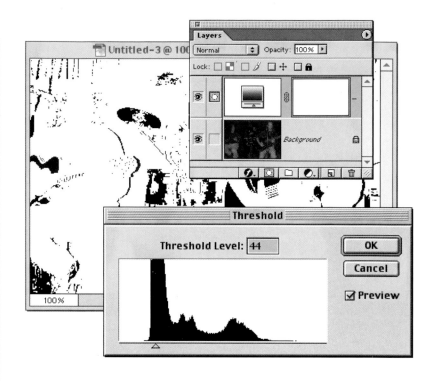

STEP TEN: Now let's mark your shadow point for later use. You do this by going to the Toolbox and clicking-and-holding on the Eyedropper tool. When you do, a menu will "fly out" where you can choose the Color Sampler tool. (This tool was introduced back in Photoshop 5.0, and it lets you place up to four different Eyedroppers and get a reading for each. We're not going to use this feature of the Color Sampler tool; we're only using it as a marker or placeholder.) Choose this tool, then click once on the area that is darkest (I clicked on the left side of his guitar). When you do this, a target icon will appear on that spot, marking it for future reference. Also, the Info palette will automatically pop up. We're not going to use the Info palette in this technique, so you can click to close it, or move it to one side so it's out of the way.

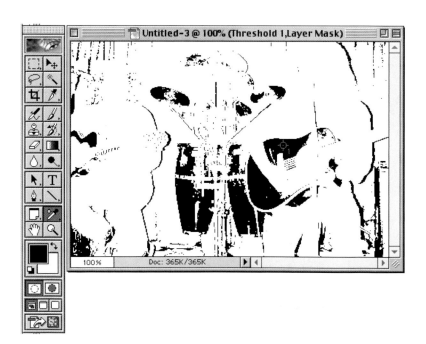

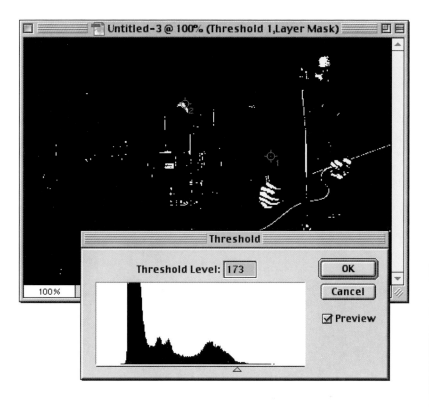

STEP ELEVEN: Go back to the Layers palette and double-click on the Threshold Adjustment Layer icon to once again bring up the Threshold dialog box. Drag the Threshold Level slider all the way to the right. Your image will turn black. Slowly drag the Threshold slider back to the left, and as you do, you'll start to see some of your bitmapped image reappear. The first thing that appears is the lightest part of your image. Again, this is Photoshop telling you exactly where the lightest part of the image is. Click OK in the Threshold dialog, then take the Color Sampler tool and click once on the brightest point (white point) to mark it for reference. The guitarist's forehead and hands are among the brightest areas, but I know they're not supposed to be white. There's a clamp on the percussion setup that appears (in the original image) to be solid white, so I clicked the Color Sampler on that instead.

STEP TWELVE: In the Layers palette, drag the Threshold Adjustment layer into the Trash at the bottom of the Layers palette to delete it. When you do this, you'll see your image reappear in color, but you'll notice there are now two target markers. The first one is named #1 and is your shadow (black) point. The other is named #2 and is your highlight (white) point. (In the image shown here, the #1 sampler is on the guitar. The #2 sampler is just to the left of the cymbal in the center of the image.)

STEP THIRTEEN: Bring back the Curves dialog box by pressing Command-M (PC: Control-M) and click once on the shadow Eyedropper. Move your cursor outside the Curves dialog box into your image and click once directly on the center of the #1 target. When you click on the #1 target, you'll see the colors shift on screen to reflect your new shadow point. Often, you'll see a dramatic difference, especially if your image had a major color cast in the shadow areas. If you click and your image looks absolutely horrible or the colors shift to obviously wrong colors, you can undo your change by pressing Command-Z (PC: Control-Z). You can then try clicking in another shadow area. Don't let it discourage you, though, if the first spot you choose isn't exactly right, just use that undo shortcut and try again until it looks right. When it does—don't click OK yet—go on to the next step.

STEP FOURTEEN: While still in the Curves dialog box, click once on the highlight (white point) Eyedropper. Move your cursor over your image, and click once directly on the center of the #2 target to assign your highlight point. You'll see the colors shift on screen, and now, most of the color casts should be removed from your image. It should look brighter and crisper, and the colors should appear much more like the original image. You can now remove the two Color Sampler targets by holding the Option key (PC: Alt key) and clicking once directly on each color sampler to remove them from your image (it will not affect the colors in your image when you remove these samplers). Then, in the Curves dialog box, click on the center of the curve and drag slightly upward to brighten the midtones of the image (as shown bottom right).

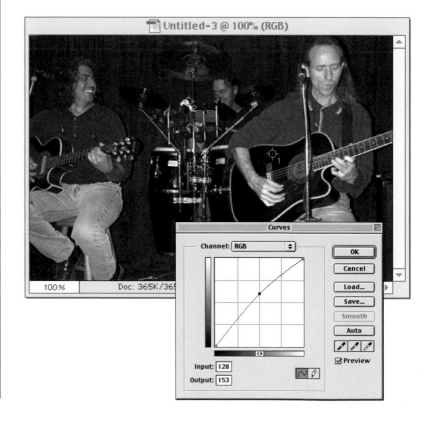

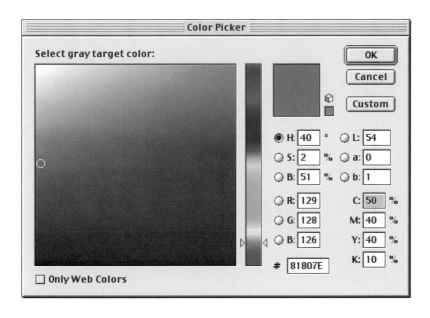

The original image (at left)

STEP FIFTEEN: What if you've set the white and black points but there's still a color cast? While setting the highlight and shadows will usually do the trick, sometimes there's a color cast in the midtones. To remove a midtone cast, go back to the Curves dialog and double-click on the midtone Eyedropper (it's the center one). Enter 50 for cyan, 40 for magenta, 40 for yellow, and 10 for black. Click OK. Here's another tricky part—click this Eyedropper on an area in the image that is supposed to be neutral gray. I know, I know, there may not be a part of the image that's supposed to be gray—that's what makes this part so tricky. If you click and it looks horrible, you probably clicked in the wrong spot. Undo it and try again until it looks right. (I clicked on some gray hardware, just above the congas, to remove the midtone color cast.)

STEP SIXTEEN: Well, that's a quick look at removing color casts in RGB mode. However, if you're going to a printing press, you have another problem to deal with—flesh tones. We'll tackle that next. But before we do that, on the next page is a look at another quick technique for finding highlight and shadow points. You can never have too many, ya know.

QUICK TIPS

You can get the Color Sampler tool while you're in the Levels or Curves dialog boxes by holding the Shift key.

Another Quick Trick for Finding Highlight and Shadow Points in your Image

In the previous technique, we looked at how to use a Threshold Adjustment Layer to pinpoint the shadow and highlight areas in your image. If you don't feel like going through all those steps, this simple technique, using the Info palette, might be just what you're looking for.

STEP ONE: Go under the Window menu and choose Show Info to make the Info palette visible. In the Info palette, by default, the top left reading shows the RGB color values. Click-and-hold on the little Eyedropper icon on the top left and a pop-up list of measurement options will appear. Choose Total Ink.

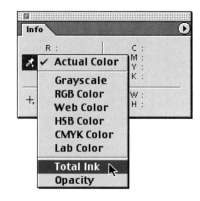

STEP TWO: Move the Eyedropper tool over the dark areas of your image. As you do this, look at the Info palette's first field, and it will display the total amount of ink in that area. Look for the highest number you can. When you find approximately the highest number, that's the darkest part of the image.

Use this same method to find the highlight (white point). Look for approximately the lowest number you can find, and that will be the highlight. However, try to find a highlight that has some detail, and avoid choosing what are called "specular highlights" (e.g., reflections on chrome, the sun, etc.).

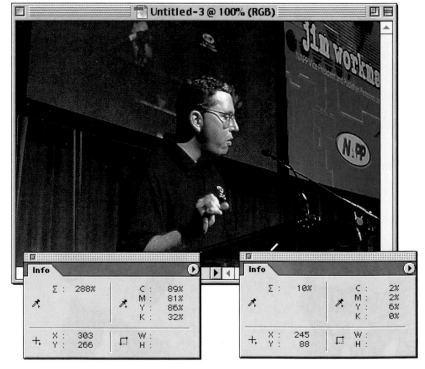

The highest amount of ink found in the image can be used as the shadow point (288%, shown top left of dialog).

The lowest amount of ink found in the image can be used as the highlight point (10%, shown top left of dialog).

Adjusting Flesh Tones for CMYK Printing

When you're correcting images that will be printed on a printing press, you don't want anything in the image to jump out and tell the person viewing the image "hey, this wasn't color-corrected properly." Unless something is horribly wrong, it usually won't be the sky or the grass that "jumps out." There is one area that, if not corrected properly, *is* a dead giveaway—flesh tones. Here's the secret to getting perfect flesh tones on press, by correcting "by the numbers."

STEP ONE: Before you can correct the flesh tones, and before you can go to press, you'll have to convert your image from RGB mode to CMYK mode. Although the conversion from RGB to CMYK is as easy as choosing CMYK from the Mode submenu, don't do it. At least not yet. First, you should call the print shop that's printing your job and get their CMYK separation setup *before* you make that conversion. That way you'll get the best possible separation for their particular printing press (yes, it makes a difference).

If you can't get a hold of the print shop, don't know which print shop will actually be printing the job (if you're collaborating with other people on this project), or if you just don't want to call the print shop, you can use Photoshop's default CMYK settings and nothing bad will happen to your image. Photoshop's default settings will provide a safe, average-looking separation, but you can get much better-looking separations by using the custom settings from the print shop printing the job, so why not make the call?

Once you have input the custom settings into your Custom CMYK dialog box (choose Color Settings under the Edit menu and when the Color Settings dialog box appears, in the Working Spaces section, choose Custom CMYK in the CMYK pop-up menu, as shown at right), *then* you can go under the Image menu, under Mode, and choose CMYK Color.

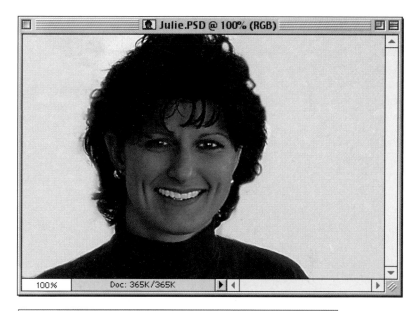

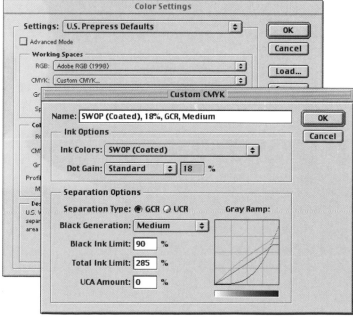

STEP TWO: Go under the Window menu and choose Show Info. This brings up the Info palette, which you'll use in conjunction with Curves to adjust your flesh tones. As you move your cursor around in your image, the Info palette gives you the RGB values and CMYK values for the area directly under your cursor. When it comes to flesh tones on a printing press, you're only concerned with the relationship between the magenta and the yellow in the flesh tone areas. The secret to getting proper flesh tones on press is this—you need to adjust the image so that there's at least 3% to 5% more yellow than magenta in the flesh tone areas. In fact, a number of prepress pros shoot for 10% more yellow. The next step will show you how to make this simple adjustment.

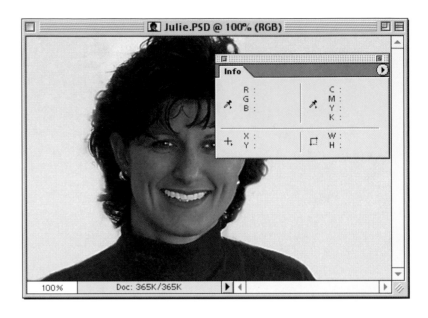

STEP THREE: The first thing you need to do is get a reading from the flesh tone in your image. You can do this without the Curves dialog being open, but you're going to be making changes there anyway, so press Command-M (PC: Control-M) to open it now. Next, move your cursor outside the Curves dialog box and into your image. Move your cursor over an area of your image that contains flesh tones (we'll call this our sample area). While your cursor is there, look in your Info palette at the relationship of the magenta and the yellow. If the magenta value is higher than the yellow value (which is often the case), you'll have to adjust the balance of the magenta and the yellow. In the image here, the magenta in the sample area of the flesh tone is 14% higher than the yellow, signaling that a flesh tone adjustment is necessary.

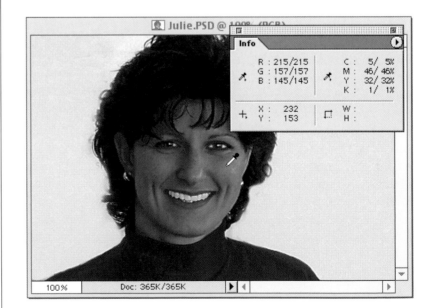

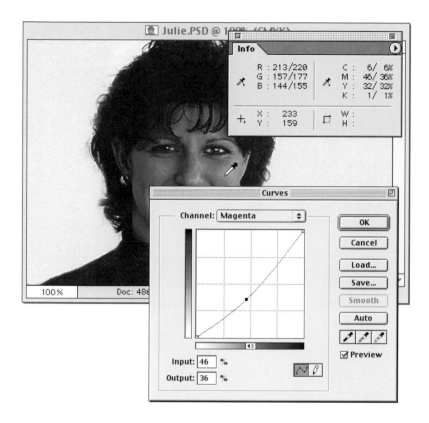

STEP FOUR: We make the adjustment in two steps: (1) We decrease the amount of magenta in the flesh tones and (2) add yellow to balance it out. First, let's adjust the magenta. To find out exactly where the magenta is in your flesh tone sample area, in the Curves dialog, choose Magenta from the Channel pop-up menu. Hold the Command key (PC: Control key) and click once in the sample flesh tone area. This adds a point to the magenta channel curve right where the magenta in the flesh tone is located. Click on this point and drag downward to decrease the amount of magenta. Then, move your cursor over the sample area again and get another reading. You get a before/after reading with your original value on the left and your adjusted value on the right.

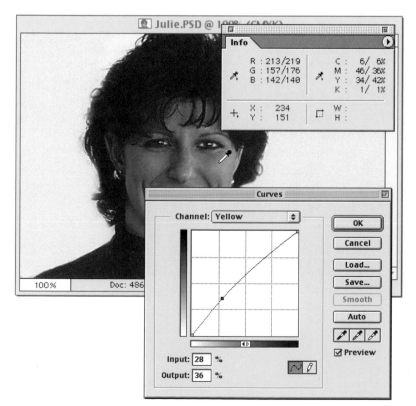

STEP FIVE: Once you have the magenta lowered, you'll need to switch to the Yellow channel by choosing it from the Channel pop-up menu at the top of the Curves dialog. Again, you'll hold the Command key (PC: Control key) and click once on the sample flesh tone area, and this will add a point to your yellow channel curve right where the yellow resides in the sample flesh tone area. This time, you'll drag upward to add yellow to your flesh tone. You'll need to increase the amount of yellow until the average reading in that area has the yellow at least 3% higher than the magenta (in our example, I lowered the magenta to 36% and raised the Yellow to 42%).

STEP SIX: Chances are your image looks a bit yellow on screen, and the people themselves may look a bit jaundiced. Don't worry, when it comes to going to press, you can't trust what you see on screen. Yes, it is too yellow, but that will go away on press. If you corrected by the numbers, you can rest assured that your correction will yield flesh tones that look natural when printed on a printing press. Now the next step is for people who *aren't* going to press.

STEP SEVEN: OK, what if you're not going to press? You've done the basic corrections from the previous technique, "Removing Color Casts," and for some strange reason, your flesh tones still don't look right. I say "some strange reason" because your basic corrections should have removed any weird color casts, and your flesh tones on screen should look pretty good. Think of it this way: If the grass looks green and the sky looks blue, it's unlikely the people in your image have a bright green flesh tone. If the colors on screen look good everywhere else, it's unlikely that your flesh tones have somehow snuck by your earlier corrections; but just in case... there are also RGB values you can target using the Info palette.

STEP EIGHT: A reasonable target value for RGB flesh tones is to have the Red value approximately 50% higher than the Green value, and to have the Green value about 20% higher than the Blue value. Luckily, if you're not going to press, you don't have to worry about the relationship between the magenta and yellow inks (especially since you're in RGB mode). That's because we're only worried about that relationship when the inks interact on a CMYK printing press. Look at the RGB readings for this image. The Red is about 35% higher than the Green, which is only about 10% higher than the Blue. If I were going to make an adjustment, I would lower the amount of blue (in Curves, the same way we made the CMYK adjustments—only it will be on the Blue channel instead of Cyan) so there's about a 20% difference between the blue and green. You could add in a bit of red, but I probably wouldn't bother.

STEP NINE: The flesh tone image at left probably doesn't look right, and it shouldn't. It's an RGB screen capture meant for output to a color inkjet printer. However, we had to print it in the book, so here it's a CMYK image separated as a screen capture (not a photograph), so it should look a bit funky in print.

Turn the page for another technique for correcting RGB values for flesh tones.

QUICK TIPS

To open/close the Info palette, press F8.

Adjusting RGB Flesh Tones

After removing the color casts (using the methods shown earlier in this chapter), you may still have a problem with the flesh tones being too red. This is especially likely if the images were scanned in, rather than coming from a digital camera (although some digital cameras do introduce a magenta/red cast in the flesh tones as well). Here's one way to deal with it.

STEP ONE: Open the corrected RGB image containing flesh tones that appear too red (incidentally, although we're removing red using this technique, if you have an image that has too much blue, or too much green, this simple technique will also work. You'll soon see in this technique where you can make a slight change for blue or green problems). If the whole image appears too red, continue on to the next step. If the red is just in the flesh tone areas, use the Lasso tool to make a selection around those areas. Hold the Shift key to add other flesh tone areas to the selection, such as hands, arms, legs, etc. Then go under the Select menu and choose Feather. Enter a Feather Radius of 1 pixel, then click OK.

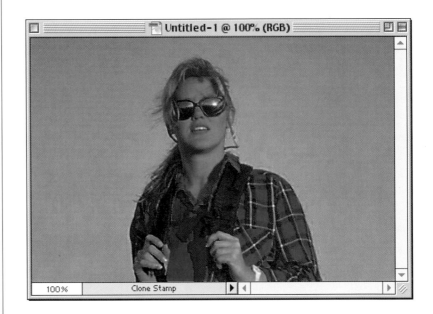

STEP TWO: Go under the Image Menu, under Adjust, and choose Hue/Saturation. When the dialog box appears, it's set to edit the Master (overall) color of the image by default. Click-and-hold on the Edit pop-up menu and choose Reds. (Note: If your flesh tones appear too yellow or too blue, here's where you would choose that color instead.)

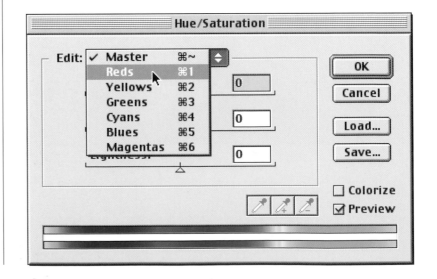

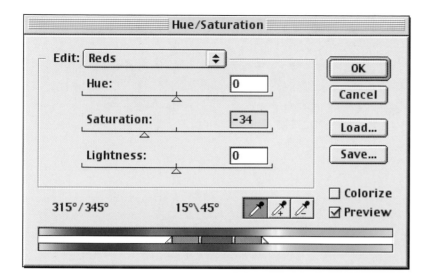

STEP THREE: What you're going to do here is quite simple—you're going to reduce the saturation of the red so the flesh tone appears more normal. Click-and-drag the Saturation slider to the left to reduce the amount of red in the image (if you selected any flesh tone areas before opening this dialog, this change will only affect those areas). If the preview box is checked, you'll be able to see the effect on the image of removing the red as you lower the Saturation slider. TIP: If you make a selection of the flesh tone areas, you can hide the selection border from view, making it easier to see what you're affecting, by pressing Command-H (PC: Control-H), even while the Hue/Saturation dialog box is open.

STEP FOUR: When you click OK, the flesh tones in your image will have less red and will look more natural.

In the previous sections, we uncovered the secret for getting proper flesh tones on a printing press, and here, we briefly looked at correcting RGB flesh tone values. When you turn the page, we'll tackle one of the most important issues in creating crisp, clean images: sharpening.

QUICK TIPS

The keyboard shortcut to bring up the Hue/Saturation dialog box is Command-U (PC:Control-U).

Sharpening Images

Every image you capture, whether from a scanner, digital camera, or Photo CD, loses some of the sharpness of the original image, and that's why having the ability to sharpen these images is so important. Photoshop's Unsharp Mask filter is the industry's sharpening workhorse and this tutorial will show you how and when to apply it to bring the sharp, crisp look back to your images.

STEP ONE: In Photoshop, it's best to apply sharpening as the very last step just before saving the file. Sharpening has a pretty significant effect on the pixels in the image, so once you've sharpened in Photoshop, you really don't want to go back and tweak the image. Generally, sharpening is the last thing we do before saving. I'm going to assume you've followed the steps earlier in this chapter and have already color-corrected the image and lowered the resolution for final output. Your retouching tasks are done, and now it's time to sharpen and save the file.

STEP TWO: The pro's tool for sharpening is the Unsharp Mask filter, which is found under the Filter menu, under Sharpen. You could simply apply Unsharp Mask to your entire RGB composite image and probably be just fine, but there is a danger because applying the filter to your entire image can cause color shifts, halos, and other nasties in your image. That's why most pros don't apply the Unsharp Mask to the RGB image. Instead, they convert to Lab Color mode and then apply the sharpening to the luminosity of the image, and not to the color channels. To start, go under the Image menu, under Mode, and choose Lab Color.

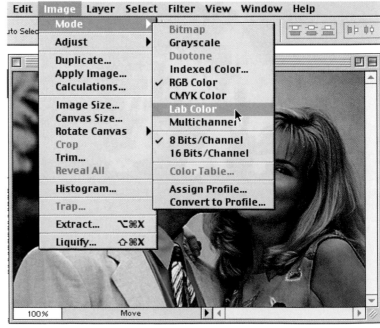

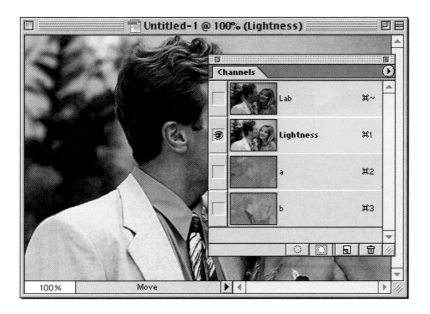

STEP THREE: Unlike converting to CMYK mode, converting to Lab Color does not damage or throw away any colors in your image, so moving from RGB to Lab is a very safe conversion. Once you've made the conversion, go to the Window menu and choose Show Channels to bring up the Channels palette. In the Channels palette, click on the Lightness channel. This channel contains the luminosity of the image (and the "a" and "b" channels contain the color info), so applying the sharpening here avoids potential problems with color shifts and thus enables you to add more sharpening than you normally would in RGB mode.

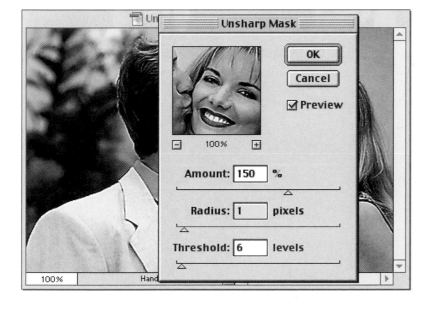

STEP FOUR: When you make the Lightness channel active, you'll see a grayscale image on screen. Don't let that throw you. Now it's time to apply the Unsharp Mask filter. Go under the Filter menu, under Sharpen, and choose Unsharp Mask. When the dialog box appears, there are three sliders for adjusting how the filter is applied. The Amount slider controls (not surprisingly) the amount of sharpening. The Radius determines how many pixels the filter will affect and is usually set to either 1 or .5 (half) a pixel. In certain situations, the Radius may be raised as high as 4, but generally, it's in the 1-pixel range. The Threshold slider determines which pixels to sharpen based on their difference with surrounding pixels. If the pixel is in the Threshold range, it is considered an edge pixel and will be sharpened.

STEP FIVE: Rather than making you hunt and peck to find out which settings work best, I'm going to give you some of my favorite settings—settings that I shamelessly stole from a number of leading scanning experts (don't tell them I told you or I'd get in big trouble). So here they are, the way-cool settings and when to use them. The first setting (Amount: 150, Radius: 1, Threshold: 10) is ideal when the subject of your image is of a softer nature (such as shots of people, flowers, etc.) because the amount of sharpening is very subtle. The second set of settings (Amount: 85, Radius: 1, Threshold: 4), my personal favorite, works on most images and has a more pronounced effect, yet doesn't appear too harsh.

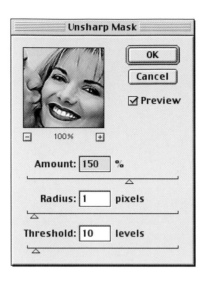

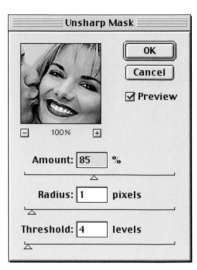

STEP SIX: The next two sets of settings are much more intense and are used in the following two instances: (1) When the subject of the image is primarily made up of objects with well-defined edges (such as buildings, coins, cars, etc.), and (2) when the image is visibly blurry and needs sharpening to make the image acceptable. Try both of the settings shown at right, starting with the one on the left and then the one on the right and see which amount of sharpening appeals to you (the one on the right is the more intensive of the two). The best way to find out which of these four settings is right for you is to try them on various images. You'll probably find one or two of them that suit your eye and you'll wind up sticking with those most of the time, rather than trying to calculate a separate setting for each image (life is too short for that).

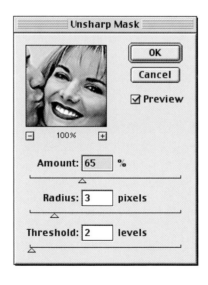

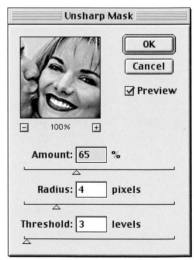

STEP SEVEN: After you've chosen which settings look best (you do get an on-screen preview if the preview checkbox is checked), click OK to apply the filter to the Lightness channel. (I applied the filter with the settings 85, 1, 4 to the image shown here.)

STEP EIGHT: If you apply the sharpening and it doesn't look sharp enough, rather than undoing the filter and experimenting with different settings, run the Unsharp Mask filter again using the same settings by pressing Command-F (PC: Control-F). This will usually do the trick. Although most times you'll only need to apply it once, there will be instances where two applications of the filter with the same settings adds the right amount of sharpening. (The image shown here had the filter applied twice, both times using 85, 1, 4.)

STEP NINE: So what happens if you apply the filter once and it's not quite enough sharpening, but when you apply it a second time, it's a bit too much? Well, you can "Fade" the filter. The best way I can describe the Fade command is it acts as an "undo on a slider." Here's how to use it: Once you've applied the filter (in this case, the second application of the filter) and it appears over-sharpened (and in this image, I feel it is a bit over-sharpened), you can go under the Edit menu and choose Fade Unsharp Mask. This brings up a dialog box with an Opacity slider. When you drag the slider to the left, the amount of the Unsharp Mask filter you last applied will be lowered. In this case, I lowered the intensity to 61% of the last application of the filter. When it looks good, click OK.

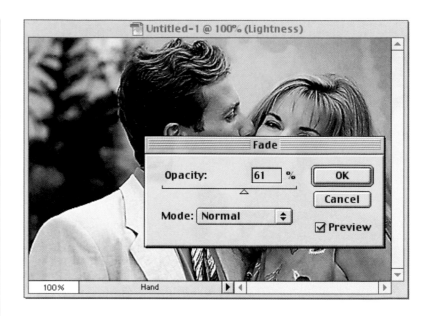

STEP TEN: When you're finished sharpening, you can go back under the Image menu, under Mode, and choose RGB Color to convert back to RGB mode and see the final effects of your sharpening.

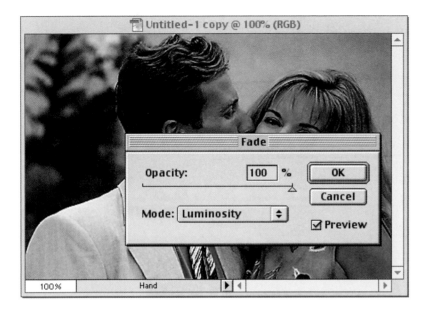

STEP ELEVEN: There's another sharpening technique that's gaining popularity: applying the Unsharp Mask filter to the image in RGB mode and using the Fade filter's blend mode to apply the filter to just the luminance channel. Here's how: Apply the Unsharp Mask filter, then go under the Edit menu and choose Fade Unsharp Mask. When the dialog box appears, don't lower the Opacity—instead, change the blend Mode from Normal to Luminosity, then click OK. Doing it in this fashion applies the filter to just the Luminosity of the image, which helps avoid the common problems of applying it to the RGB image as a whole.

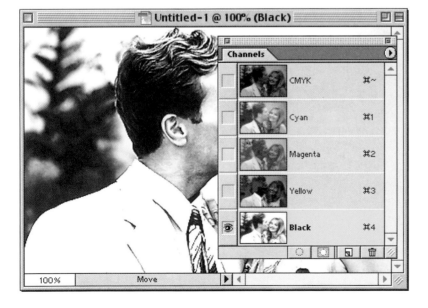

STEP TWELVE: There's yet another technique if your image is already in CMYK mode. Go to the Channels palette and click on the Black channel. Now, apply the Unsharp Mask filter to just the Black channel. Treat this just like you would if you were applying it to the Lab Color Lightness channel (by that I mean apply the filter, twice if necessary, and then use Fade).

QUICK TIPS

The shortcut to bring up the Fade dialog box is Shift-Command-F (PC: Shift-Control-F).

Color Retouching One Area

You've probably run across this situation dozens of times (if not, you will) where the overall image looks good, but you wish part of it looked better (e.g., the sky isn't as blue as you'd like or the grass looks kind of brown instead of green). You could select the sky, add feather, and use Curves or Levels to tweak just those colors, but you really have to have a good understanding of color correction. That's why this trick is so cool—you can fix that sky, grass, etc., in just a few seconds with no prior color-correction experience.

STEP ONE: Open an image that has an area that needs some color punch. In this case, the overall image looks good, but the sky and the creek look kind of gray, lifeless, and bland. Since most of the image looks pretty good, we're just going to adjust the sky, and since it's blue, the little creek will be enhanced as well (as it reflects the color of the sky).

STEP TWO: Go to the Layers palette and choose Color Balance from the Adjustment Layer pop-up menu at the bottom of the Layers palette (it's the black and white circle icon, fourth from the left). A new Color Balance Adjustment Layer will appear in the Layers palette (it looks like a square icon with a circle and triangle inside it and a slider beneath). If you expand your Layers palette out far enough to the right, you can actually see the name "Color Balance" beside the layer thumbnails.

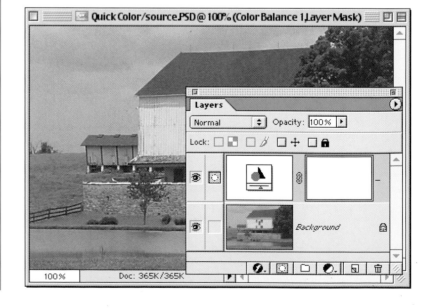

STEP THREE: When you add the Color Balance Adjustment Layer, the Color Balance dialog box will appear. Drag the Blue slider all the way to the right, giving the entire image a heavy blue tint. If the blue appears too deep (and in this case it does), add in some cyan by dragging the Cyan slider to the left.

STEP FOUR: Press the "d" key to switch your foreground color to black. Switch to the Paintbrush tool, choose a large, soft-edged brush, and paint away the blue tint that appears over the barn, the wall, the trees and the grass. Basically, it erases the blue tint, so paint over every area that shouldn't be tinted blue. If you accidentally erase part of the sky color, or the creek color, just press the "x" key to make white your foreground, and then you can paint the blue tint right back in. If you set your foreground to 50% gray, it will paint a 50/50 mix of the original and the blue color. When you're done (it takes just a minute or two) the image will look like the one shown here—with an enhanced sky and creek.

CHAPTER SIX

Quite honestly, this isn't the most exciting chapter in the book, so I had to give it a tough name so you'd

Scared Straight
cropping and straightening images

actually consider reading it. Look, I know that you don't want to read a chapter on cropping—nobody does. That's why I added the whole "straightening images" section, to sweeten the deal. But down deep, at places you don't talk about at parties, you want to read this chapter; you need to read this chapter.

Actually, although this may not sound like an exciting chapter, you'll probably use the techniques found here more often than the techniques you actually bought the book for. Ah, the heck with it. Even I can't make this chapter sound exciting. It's cropping for goodness sake! I had to include it in the book, and yes you should definitely read it 'cause it's got some important stuff in it. But you're not going to, are you? And therein lies the problem. Cropping chapters don't sell books. There— I said it (I feel much better now).

Cropping Techniques

Cropping is an amazingly useful tool in retouching, and there are a couple of different ways to crop an image in Photoshop. It's important to understand what happens when you crop an image or move an image off the canvas. In this short tutorial, we'll look at three different cropping techniques.

CROPPING TECHNIQUE #1

STEP ONE: Open an image that you want to crop.

STEP TWO: Press the "c" key to switch to the Crop tool. (Back in Photoshop 5.0 and 5.5, the Crop tool was hidden behind the Marquee Selection tools, and when you pressed the "c" key, it appeared in place of the Marquee Selection tool.)

STEP THREE: Click-and-drag the Crop tool over the area in your image you want to *keep*. You can adjust the Crop tool boundary by clicking and dragging on the handles that appear on the corners and sides of the boundary. You can also rotate this boundary by moving your cursor outside the crop selection. When you do this, your cursor will change into a two-headed arrow enabling you to rotate by just clicking and dragging in the direction you want to rotate.

STEP FOUR: When you have the cropping boundary where you want, press Return (PC: Enter) to crop your image to fit inside the boundary. The rest of the image is discarded. There's another way to crop shown in the next technique.

QUICK TIPS

When you use the Crop tool, it automatically dims the areas to be cropped away. You can adjust the color and the opacity of the dimmed area in the Options Bar.

CROPPING TECHNIQUE #2

STEP ONE: You can also crop without using the Crop tool at all. Try this: Switch to the Rectangular Marquee tool and draw a selection inside your image (it doesn't matter where you place your selection, just make sure it's at least 1" inside the current image border, so when you crop, you can see the results).

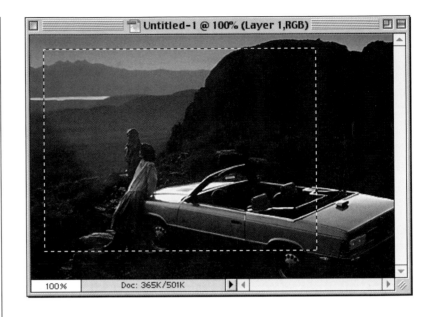

STEP TWO: Go under the Image menu and choose Crop. The image is cropped to fit within your selected area and the rest of the image is discarded. This is fine for making a simple crop, but it doesn't give you the flexibility of the Crop tool because you can't rotate the selection and still crop, and you can't easily resize the border before you crop. The next technique shows yet another way to crop an image.

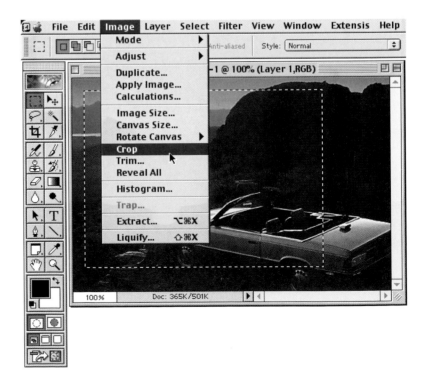

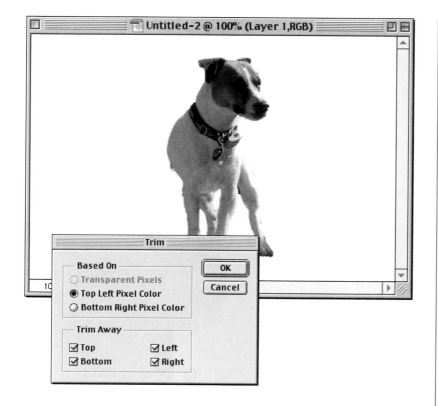

CROPPING TECHNIQUE #3

STEP ONE: This is the cropping technique where you let Photoshop do all the work. It crops your image as tightly as possible, based on the parameters you enter in the Trim dialog box. To "trim" an image, go under the Image menu and choose Trim. When the dialog box appears, you can choose what you want the cropping Based On and what you want to Trim Away. The default setting will crop the object as tightly as possible and is useful when you have a background that is a solid color, as we do here.

STEP TWO: When you click OK, the image is automatically cropped to your specifications (at least the ones you entered in the Trim dialog box). This technique is particularly important if you're creating Web graphics and you need the tightest crop possible for the smallest possible file size.

Cropping to Repair Barrel Distortion

Photoshop 6.0 is the first version of Photoshop to have a built-in function for repairing distortions created by the lens of a camera. Barrel distortion or "fall-away" distortion is often found in images with buildings or tall objects. The buildings look like they're falling away from the viewer, meaning their tops are more narrow than their bases. Fixing these distortions in Photoshop is accomplished using the Crop tool and its Perspective function.

STEP ONE: Open an image that has a lens distortion problem. Then, switch to the Crop tool by pressing the "c" key. Click-and-drag out a cropping border around your entire image (or just the particular area that you want to crop down to).

STEP TWO: You're going to use the Perspective feature of Photoshop's Crop tool. When you use this feature, you can extend the crop handles beyond the image outside into the canvas area. In the Toolbox, locate the second set of icons from the bottom and click on the middle one. This will center your image on screen, revealing the gray canvas background so you can work with your cropping border. When your Crop selection is in place, go to the Options Bar and click on the checkbox named Perspective.

STEP THREE: Once the Perspective option is turned on, you can grab any of the corner points and drag outward into the gray canvas area to offset the amount of lens distortion. Once you have it in position, press Return (PC: Enter) to lock in your crop. Now, you're about to encounter two problems: (1) you're pretty much doing this blind, since the Crop tool doesn't give you a preview as you drag the handles, and (2) this is one finicky tool. Sometimes it will let you perform the perspective crop, but most often you'll get the error message "The center point is not correctly placed or the corners are not properly selected." What's that mean? Who knows? Read on to the next step for a workaround.

STEP FOUR: The workaround for this Crop madness is to not use the Crop tool at all. Instead, use Free Transform, which gives you a preview of what you're doing and never generates an error message. Here's how: Press Command-A (PC: Control-A) to select the entire image, then press Command-T (PC: Control-T) to bring up Free Transform. Hold the Command key (PC: Control key) and drag out different corner points until your onscreen preview looks right. The onscreen preview makes correcting distortion easy. In this example, after the Free Transform adjustment, the glass still looked "round and bloated," so I went under the Filter menu, under Distort, and chose Pinch. For Amount, I used 5% and it pinched it just right.

QUICK TIPS

When using the Crop tool, you can tell Photoshop to complete the crop by double-clicking within the cropping border.

Straightening Crooked Scans

Here's a surprisingly quick, easy, and precise way to straighten any crooked scanned image. I really don't know what else to say about this technique, but I need more text to fill up some space in this introduction area, so I hope you don't mind if I just kind of babble a bit. Thanks, that really helps a lot. See, it took up the space I needed and no one got hurt.

STEP ONE: Open the scanned image that needs straightening. Press Shift-I until the Measure tool appears in the Toolbox (it looks like a little ruler).

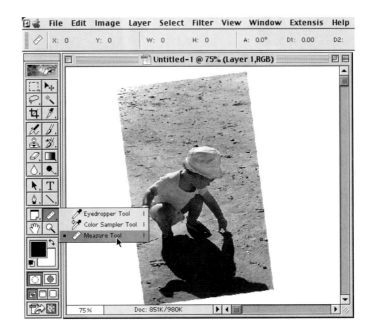

STEP TWO: Drag the Measure tool across the top edge of your image so it follows the angle of your crooked image (or find an object in the image that should be horizontal and drag the tool along its edge). As soon as you drag the tool, you can see the angle of the line in both the Info palette and the Options Bar, but you can ignore them both, because Photoshop is already taking note of the angle and placing that info where you'll need it in the next step.

STEP THREE: Go under the Image menu, under Rotate Canvas, and choose Arbitrary. Photoshop has already put the angle of rotation of the image in the dialog box for you. It also enters whether the image should be rotated Clockwise or Counterclockwise. All you have to do now is click OK, and the image will be perfectly straightened (as long as you dragged the ruler straight along the once-crooked edge).

STEP FOUR: Now that the image is straight, you can draw a rectangular selection around the image, then go under the Image menu and choose Crop, to crop the image to size.

QUICK TIPS

When using the Measure tool, if you want to clear the last measurement and remove the line it drew in your image, press the Clear button that appears in the Options Bar.

Straightening Crooked Scans Using the Grid

This is another technique for straightening images. Some people prefer this method to the one shown on the previous pages, because they feel it's easier to align to a visible grid than trying to find a straight line within the image to drag the Measure tool along. Here's how it's done:

STEP ONE: Open an image that needs straightening. Then, go under the View menu, under Show, and choose Grid.

STEP TWO: When you choose Show Grid, it puts a non-printing grid over your entire image.

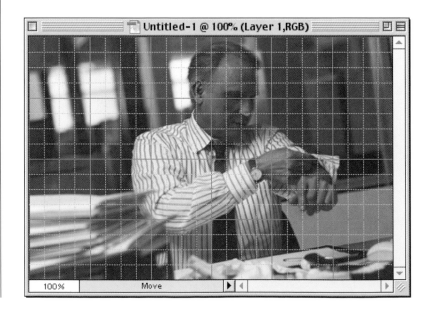

STEP THREE: The second set of icons from the bottom of the Toolbox are for setting the view of Photoshop's workspace. Click the center icon, and your image will be centered within your monitor on a gray background. Press Command-A (PC: Control-A) to select the entire image. Then, press Command-T (PC: Control-T) to bring up the Free Transform bounding box around your image. Move your cursor outside the bounding box and you'll see your cursor change into a two-headed arrow, signaling that you can now rotate the image. Look for an area within the image that is supposed to be straight, and align that part of the image to a straight line in the grid. When it looks about right, press Return (PC: Enter) to lock in your rotation.

STEP FOUR: Go back under the View menu, under Show, and choose Grid to remove the grid. Press the "m" key to switch to the Rectangular Marquee tool and draw a selection around the area of the image you want to keep. Then, go under the Image menu and choose Crop to crop the image so that none of the white areas that appeared from the rotation are visible. Your image should now be straightened.

QUICK TIPS

Once you've applied the Grid, you can toggle it on and off by pressing Command-H (PC: Control-H), which is the shortcut for Hide Extras.

Combining Images too Large to Fit on Your Scanner

What do you do when you have an image that is too wide (or too long) to fit on your scanner bed? Obviously, you buy a bigger scanner. Duh. But what if a bigger scanner is not in the budget. Or what if it's in the budget, but you need that scan today? Or what if it's in the budget, and you don't need the scan today, but you want to spend that money on a foosball table? Then here's what to do: Scan the image in sections, and then reassemble the pieces. It sounds like it would be easy, but it's harder than it might look, unless you know this slick little trick.

STEP ONE: Start by scanning the oversized image section by section, making sure each section overlaps the previous section by a least one inch. In this instance, we're going to combine two images—a left and a right scan. Use the exact same scanning settings for each image, and try to scan them both in the same area of your scanner (i.e., scan them both at the top, or both at the bottom, etc.).

STEP TWO: Open the scan that will be the left side of your image. (Note: You may need to straighten both scans so that they align perfectly. To learn how to straighten scans, check out the previous two tutorials in this chapter.) You're going to have to increase the canvas size of this image in order to accommodate adding the other scan. For example, if you scanned two 7-inch wide images, you're going to have to increase the width of your canvas size to at least 14 inches. To do this, go under the Image menu and choose Canvas Size.

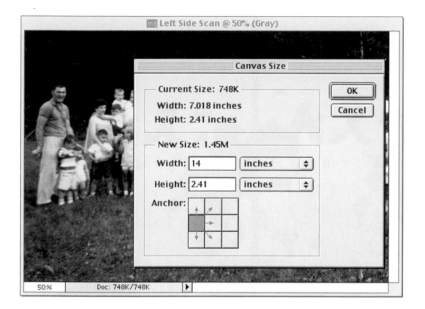

STEP THREE: When the Canvas Size dialog box appears, you'll see a grid that shows the relationship of your image to any space that you add. By default, your image is in the middle (represented in gray), and if you add any height or width, it's added on all sides. In this instance, you don't want to add any height, just width, and you only want to add it to the right of your image. To do this, click in the left, center square of the grid. Now increase the width of your image to accommodate your other scan(s). In this case, increase it to 14 inches and click OK. This adds 7 inches of white space to the right side of your image.

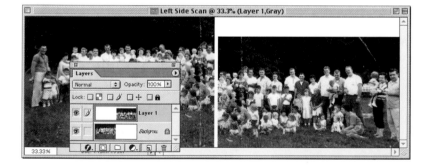

STEP FOUR: Open the other scan (the right side of your final image), and using the Move tool, drag this scan into your other document (the one you added canvas space to). When you drag this image over, it will automatically appear on its own layer above your left scan.

STEP FIVE: The key to combining these images is to find one part of the image that appears in both scans. In this case, we're going to focus on a person who appears in both scans. We're going to choose the guy who shows up just to the right of the rip in the image. If you look at the example shown at right, you'll see a man in a white T-shirt holding his daughter. As you can see, he appears on both the left scan and the right scan, so he's the guy we're going to key in on. Use the Move tool to loosely line up the two scans (not a precise alignment, just get them in the ballpark) as shown here.

STEP SIX: In the Layers palette, lower the Opacity of the right side (Layer 1) to around 60%. This enables you to see the left side of the image under the right side as you move it.

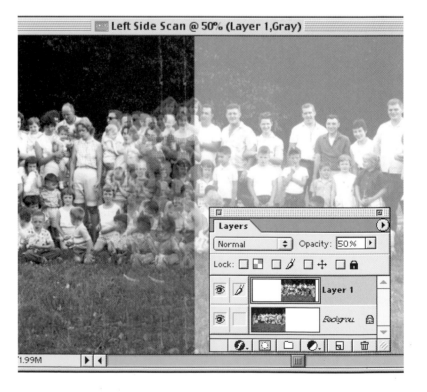

STEP SEVEN: Using the Move tool, click-and-drag the right side horizontally to the left. Look at the person you're keying in on, and continue dragging to the left until the images are about 1/2" to 1/4" from lining up.

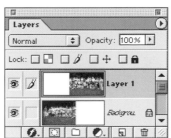

STEP EIGHT: Take your hands off the mouse at this point, and use the Arrow keys on your keyboard to nudge your right scan perfectly into place. You'll know when it's right on the money because the person you're keying in on will seem to snap into place. When that person looks right, then raise the Opacity of the right-side layer back to 100% and you're done! Now, press Command-E (PC: Control-E) to merge the two scans into one background image.

Expanding Backgrounds

Sometimes you may wind up in a situation where you actually need more background than the image has to fill in the entire canvas area (as in the example shown in Step One below). This is a quick, easy technique for expanding simple backgrounds. If it's a more complex background, you'll use this technique in combination with the Rubber Stamp tool for repeating detailed background areas.

STEP ONE: Open an image that needs more background added to fill the entire canvas area. In this example, I dragged a vertical image onto a blank horizontal document.

STEP TWO: Press the letter "m" to switch to the Rectangular Marquee tool. Make a rectangular selection of as much background (in the existing image) as you can. Then, go under the Select menu and choose Feather. For Feather Radius enter 4 pixels (enter 10 for high-res, 300-ppi images) and click OK. By softening the edges in this way, it will help hide the seam that will be created when we copy this selection and use it to fill up the missing areas of the background.

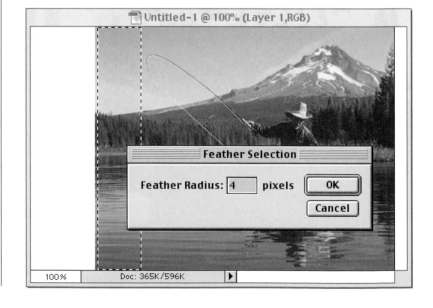

STEP THREE: Hold Shift-Command-Option (PC: Shift-Control-Alt) and drag a copy of this selection to cover the part of the image that is missing background (in this case, I dragged a copy to the left and positioned it so the seam didn't appear too obvious. Don't drag too far, or you'll see a soft-edged seam). Once you drag one copy, you can release the mouse button for a moment, and then click-and-drag other copies until the background on one side is filled. (Tip: When doing this technique, it helps if you hide the "marching ants" selection border by going under the View menu and choosing Show Extras.)

STEP FOUR: Repeat the same process on the other side: Make a selection of the background, feather the selection, and drag copies until the space is filled. If after you've dragged these copies, you see a slight seam or a repeating pattern that makes the retouch look obvious, press the letter "s" to switch to the Rubber (Clone) Stamp tool. Choose a soft-edged brush, sample in an area that doesn't have a seam, and dab over the seams until they disappear from view.

QUICK TIPS

You can have Photoshop automatically apply Feather to all your Lasso and Marquee selection tools by entering Feather values in the Options Bar of each tool.

CHAPTER SEVEN

There's only one thing that looks worse than an old, washed-out color photograph—that's right, an old,

Gray Matter
getting better grayscale images

washed-out black-and-white photograph. Back when my parents were taking baby photos of my older brother, color wasn't on the scene yet. You know what was on the scene? Crappy cameras that took crappy photos. If you're going to be working on restoring any of these vintage photos, you can remove all the spots, rips, and stains you want, but unless you can bring back all the depth, detail, and contrast that should be there, what you'll have is an old, washed-out black-and-white photo without any spots, rips, or stains.

This chapter will get you going in the right direction to bringing those lifeless, gray photos back to life. You're a life giver. A giver of life. You could easily handle a walk-on part on ER.

Correcting Grayscale Images

If you're restoring old heirloom images, you've got your hands full with fixing tears, removing spots, fixing damaged body parts, and retouching yellowing scotch tape lines. But on top of all that, the overall tone of the image is probably in pretty bad shape as well. Here's a simple step-by-step method for correcting grayscale images.

STEP ONE: Open a grayscale image that needs its overall tone adjusted.

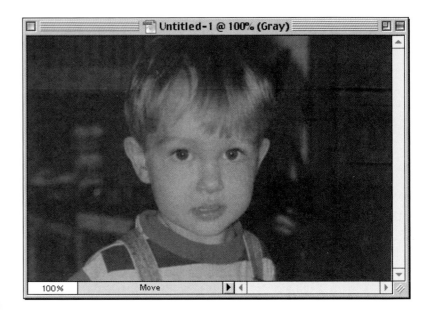

STEP TWO: Go under the Image menu, under Adjust, and choose Levels to bring up the Levels dialog box. This is where we'll make tonal adjustments using the three Input Levels sliders: the black shadow slider, the gray midtone slider, and the white highlight slider. The mountain range-like graph above the input sliders is called a Histogram, and it gives a visual readout of what Photoshop sees tonally within the image. The graph shown here has no data under or near the shadow slider (far left) and no data under or near the highlight shadow (far right). This means we have mostly a bland-looking, grayish image (all the data is in the midtone to low-midtone area) with no real shadows or highlights.

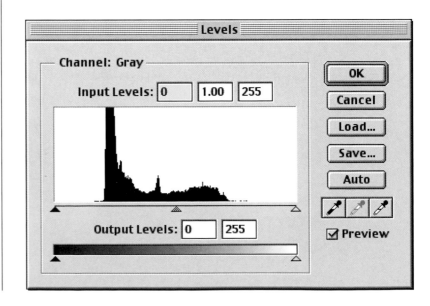

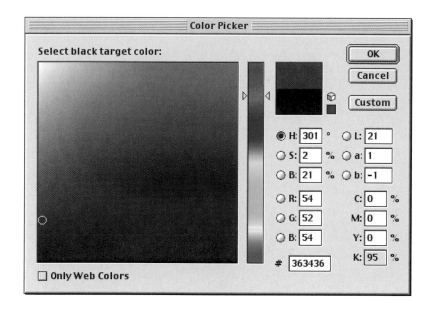

STEP THREE: Before we start correcting the image, we're going to set some Levels' preferences. There are two Eyedropper tools that reside in the Levels dialog box just below the Auto button. Double-click on the black (shadow point) Eyedropper tool on the left, and a Color Picker (that resides within the Levels dialog box) will appear asking you to "Select Black Target Color" (in other words, it wants you to select how black the darkest part of your image will be). In this case, we don't want the blacks to be so dark that there's no detail (in case we print the image out or go to press with it). So, under the CMYK fields in the bottom right-hand side of the dialog, enter C=0%, M=0%, Y=0%, K (black)=95%. Then click OK to lock in 95% as your black target Color.

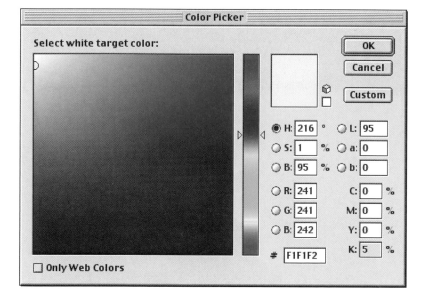

STEP FOUR: Double-click on the white (highlight point) Eyedropper tool on the right, and another Color Picker will appear asking you to "Select White Target Color" (how white you want the lightest part of your image to be). As with the black, we don't want the white to get so light that there's no detail. Again, we do this under the CMYK fields in the bottom right-hand side of the dialog. Enter C=0%, M=0%, Y=0%, K (black)=5%, and then click OK to lock in 5% as your white target Color.

QUICK TIPS

You can have Photoshop automatically correct the Levels of an image (called Auto Levels) by pressing Shift-Command-L (PC: Shift-Control-L).

STEP FIVE: For this step, the Levels dialog box should still be open. You now need to determine which part of your image is the darkest. Hold the Option key (PC: Alt key), then click-and-drag the shadow (black) Input Levels slider slowly to the right. When you do this, the image will turn white, and as you drag, the first thing that appears on screen is the darkest part of the image. Make a mental note of where that spot is (or you can use the Color Sampler tool to place a marker on that spot for future reference by holding the Shift key and clicking on that spot within your image).

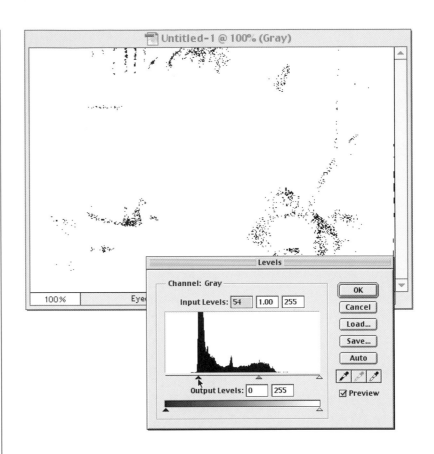

STEP SIX: Next, you'll need to determine which part of your image is the lightest. Hold the Option key (PC: Alt key), then click-and-drag the highlight (white) Input Levels slider slowly to the left. When you do this, the image will turn black, and as you drag, the first thing that appears on screen is the lightest part of the image. Make a mental note of where that spot is (or use the Color Sampler tool to mark the spot for future reference, as noted in the previous step).

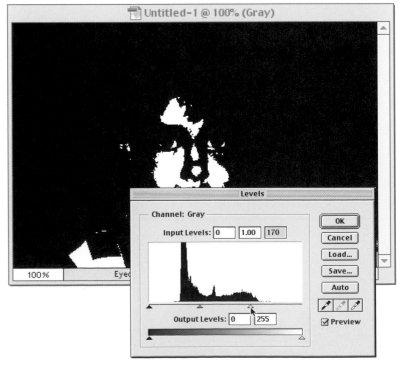

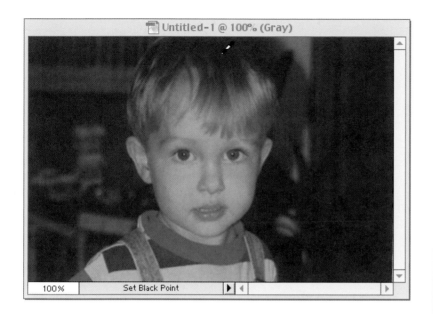

STEP SEVEN: Now that you know where the shadow and highlight points are in the image, you can assign their values. Click on the shadow (black) Eyedropper tool in the Levels dialog box, and then click once on the darkest point in the image (as determined in Step Five). Your image may appear much darker after you click using the shadow point Eyedropper.

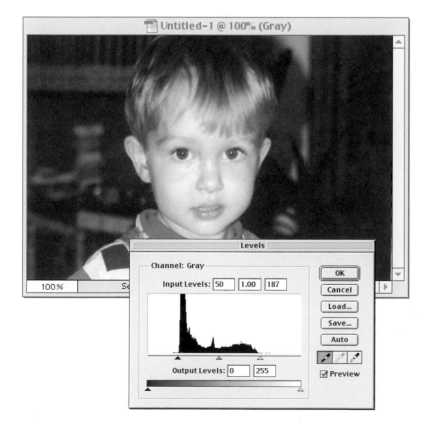

STEP EIGHT: Click on the highlight (white) Eyedropper tool in the Levels dialog box, and then click once on the lightest point in the image (as determined in Step Six). The tones in your image should start to look more balanced at this point. Note: If you click in the wrong area, don't sweat it, just press Command-Z (PC: Control-Z) to undo the last click of the Eyedropper tool, and then try again.

STEP NINE: Lastly, you'll usually want to increase the midtones (we call it "bumping the midtones"), because much of the detail in the image is contained in this area (you'll especially want to do this if you're going to press). This is a visual adjustment, and generally, we drag the slider to the left just a little bit to lighten the midtones. You'll have to use your discretion as to how far to drag the slider, but this should be a somewhat subtle adjustment. In most cases, you don't want to increase the midtone Input Level reading over 1.50 (although occasionally, you'll run across an image that breaks this rule). When the image's tone looks about right, click OK to lock in the adjustment.

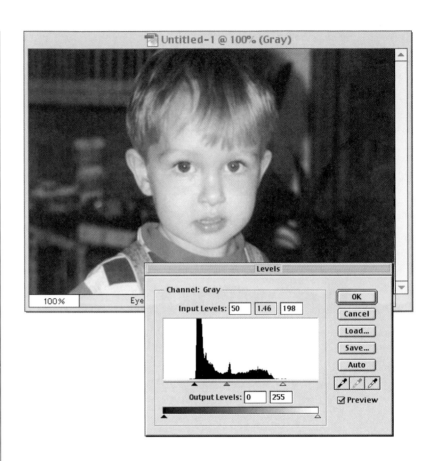

STEP TEN: To bring back some of the sharpness that is lost during the capture stage (either by scanner, digital camera, Photo CD, etc.), go under the Filter menu, under Sharpen, and choose Unsharp Mask. (Note: To learn more about sharpening, check out the "True Colors" chapter). At this stage, just enter the following sharpening values which work well for most images: Amount: 85, Radius: 1, Threshold: 4. Click OK to add this first level of sharpening.

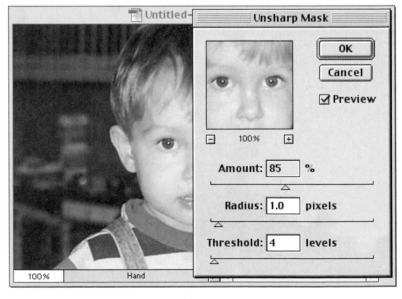

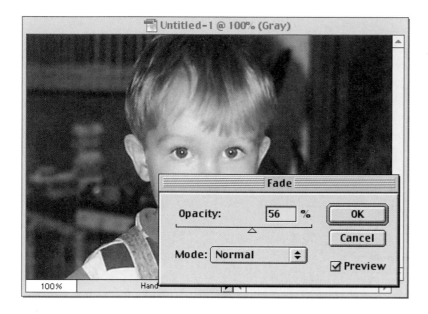

STEP ELEVEN: If you feel the image needs more sharpening, you can apply the Unsharp Mask filter again with the same settings by pressing Command-F (PC: Control-F). If the second application of the filter seems too intense, or if halos start to appear around the edges of your image, go under the Edit menu and choose Fade Unsharp Mask. When the Fade dialog box appears, use the Opacity slider as an "undo on a slider" to reduce the amount of the last application of the Unsharp Mask filter, dialing in just the right amount of sharpening.

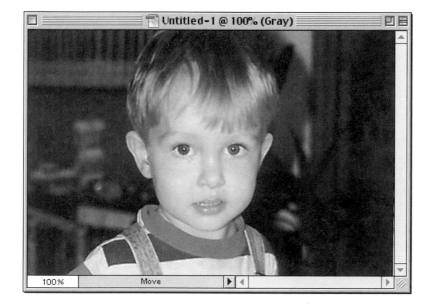

STEP TWELVE: When the adjustment with the Fade slider looks about right, click OK to complete the tonal correction for your black-and-white image. Because the image is already in grayscale, we can apply the Unsharp Mask filter directly to the image without jumping through any of the hoops that we have to with color images, because there are no color pixels to cause problems—it's all grayscale.

Tricks for Converting Color to Grayscale

Not all black-and-white images started out that way. Chances are they began as color images (from a digital camera, photo CD, or maybe even a scanner) and you had Photoshop throw away the color info, leaving you with grayscale images. But usually the grayscale images you're left with are pretty lame. There are a number of ways to coax better-looking grayscale images from Photoshop other than simply choosing "Grayscale" from the Mode menu. Here's how.

TECHNIQUE #1 (CHANNELS)

STEP ONE: For this technique to work, you have to start with a color RGB image, so open an RGB image that you want to convert to grayscale.

STEP TWO: You'll need to view the individual RGB channels of this color image, so go under the Window menu and choose Show Channels to make the Channels palette visible. When the palette appears, there's a composite RGB channel (the full color image) and individual channels for Red, Green, and Blue. These channels are displayed in grayscale, and therein lies the trick.

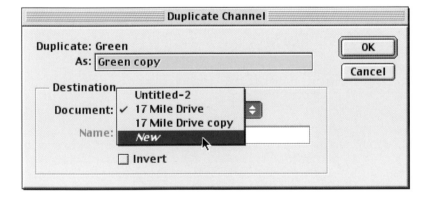

STEP THREE: Click on each individual channel and see which one looks best (when you click on the channels, they will preview on screen in grayscale). More often than not, one of these channels will actually look better than the result of just choosing Grayscale from the Mode menu. This sounds like it might be tricky—trust me, it's not. One channel will probably be way too dark (usually Blue), one will probably be a bit too light, and one channel will probably look just right (it's a three bears and porridge thing). In this case, the Green channel gave the best overall balance.

STEP FOUR: Once you've determined which channel looks best, click on the Channels palette's pop-down menu (the right-facing triangle in the upper right-hand corner) and choose Duplicate Channel. A dialog box will appear (shown here), and from the Destination pop-up menu, choose New to duplicate your chosen channel into its own separate document. Click OK and a new window will appear with your grayscale image.

QUICK TIPS

You can toggle through the individual channels by pressing Command-1, Command-2, etc. (PC: Control-1, Control-2, etc.).

STEP FIVE: Because you created this new document by copying a channel from another document, the mode of this new document will be Multichannel. You'll want to convert it to grayscale by going under the Image menu, under Mode, and choosing Grayscale. You won't see any change in the image, because it was already an 8-bit grayscale image.

STEP SIX: Once you've converted to Grayscale mode, the process is complete. Compare the image you have versus what the results would have been from a regular conversion without looking at the different channels. (Go back to your original RGB image, and then go under the Image menu, under Mode, and choose Grayscale. Now you can easily compare the two images.) Now, on to another popular color-to-grayscale conversion technique.

Standard grayscale conversion

Channel method: Notice the additional detail in the bushes, trees, and rocks, and the improved brightness and clarity of the overall image.

TECHNIQUE #2 (LAB COLOR)

STEP ONE: Open the color image you want to convert, then go under the Image menu, under Mode, and choose Lab Color.

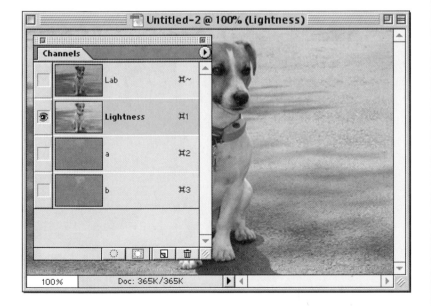

STEP TWO: Go under the Window menu and choose Show Channels to bring up the Channels palette. Click on the Lightness channel to make it active.

QUICK TIPS

Once you click on the Lightness channel, you can choose Grayscale (from the Image menu, under Mode) and Photoshop will delete the other channels for you.

STEP THREE: Just as in the previous technique, make a duplicate of the Lightness channel by going under the Channels palette's pop-up menu and choosing Duplicate Channel. When the dialog appears, choose New in the Document pop-up to have it appear in a new document by itself. Then, go under the Image menu, under Mode, and choose Grayscale for this new document.

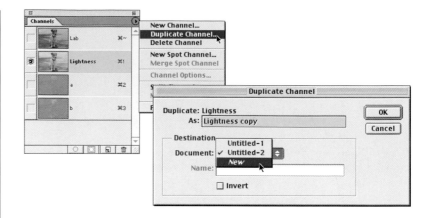

STEP FOUR: If the image appears too light (which will often be the case), go to the Layers palette and make a copy of your Background layer by dragging it to the New Layer icon at the bottom of the palette. On this copy layer, change the blend mode (from the pop-up menu in the upper left-hand corner of the palette) from Normal to Multiply. After changing the mode to Multiply, the image is now probably too dark. But you're in luck, because you can use the Opacity slider of the Multiply layer to lower the opacity and dial in the perfect blend of the two images. Try it once and you'll love it, because you have complete control.

TECHNIQUE #3 (CALCULATIONS)

STEP ONE: This is more of an advanced technique for creating the perfect grayscale image. It's not hard, but the dialog box you use looks pretty intimidating (like something NASA might use during a Shuttle launch). Start by opening the image for conversion.

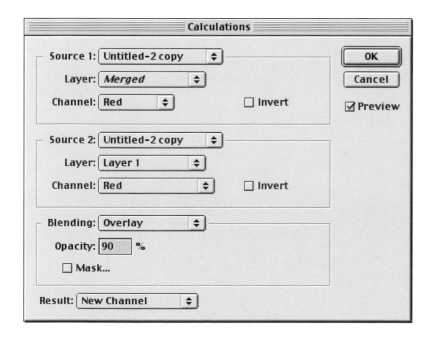

STEP TWO: Go under the Image menu and choose Calculations, and the dialog box shown here will appear. It looks complicated, but it's really not. What this dialog box lets you do is combine and blend any two channels together to create a whole new channel. So if two of the three channels look good, but one's too dark and one's too light, you can blend them together and create the perfect new channel. You can combine images from different documents (under the Source pop-up menu) or from different Layers within your document (from the Layers pop-up menu). But you're going to simply choose channels from your existing image. The cool thing is you can actually choose to blend the same channel twice (as I did here with the Red channel set to Overlay mode. I also had to lower the Opacity of the blend to 90% because it was too dark at first).

STEP THREE: Here's the same dialog again. I just need to explain it a bit more by talking you through some of the decisions I made for this example. OK, so I chose two Red channels, and it looked pretty good (you can see the results onscreen because the Preview checkbox is turned on). The default Blending mode is Multiply, which made the new channel it was creating too dark, so I went to the Blending mode pop-up menu and tried all the different modes until I came up with one that looked good. The image seemed to look best in Overlay mode—but it was just too dark, so I kept lowering the Opacity until it looked right. Then, in the pop-up menu for Result (destination), I chose New Document (like we did in the Duplicate Channel dialog box), and it created a new document with my shiny new channel. Again, I converted the image to Grayscale mode by going under the Image menu, under Mode, and choosing Grayscale.

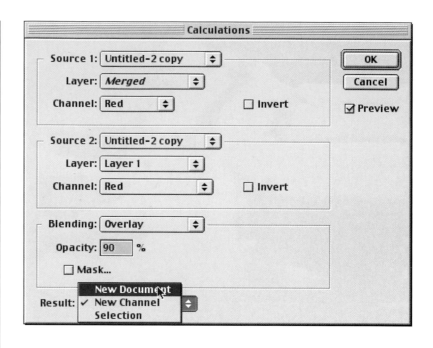

STEP FOUR: There really is no Step Four. I just wanted to show the difference between Photoshop performing the conversion (by choosing Grayscale from the Mode submenu) and your doing it using Calculations. The difference in detail is pretty obvious (at least it was onscreen—I'm hoping the detail held in print here in the book, but since it's just a screen capture, I'm not taking any bets).

Converted by choosing Grayscale from the Mode menu.

Converted using Calculations.

TECHNIQUE #4 (CHANNEL MIXER)

STEP ONE: Hard to believe but there's yet another method you can use for converting to grayscale called Channel Mixer. It lets you produce a similar effect to Calculations by blending different channels to create an ultra channel, but you don't have the blending control you do with Calculations. To get to the Channel Mixer, go under the Image menu, under Adjust, and choose Channel Mixer.

STEP TWO: In the Channel Mixer dialog box, click the Monochrome checkbox at the bottom of the dialog box to blend channels as grayscale. You can combine the channels using the sliders, and adjust the overall brightness of the image using the Constant slider near the bottom of the dialog. I have to admit, I personally don't like this method, because it takes too much experimenting (sliding) to get a decent image. I feel like I have more control, and more options, in the other techniques, but hey that's just me. The other bad thing about Channel Mixer is it doesn't give you a Grayscale document. When you click OK, you're still in RGB mode, and you still have to convert to Grayscale. The important thing is that you now know all four methods, and you can choose which one suits you best.

Creating Duotones

In many cases black-and-white images lack the depth of color images (unless Ansel Adams is taking the shots). That's one reason duotones have become popular. A duotone image is made up of black ink and one spot color. This extra color is primarily used to add depth. It's also used when the budget for a print job doesn't allow for four-color process printing. Here's how to create duotones for print.

STEP ONE: Open a grayscale image that you want to convert to a duotone.

STEP TWO: Go under the Image menu, under Mode, and choose Duotone. By default this dialog opens up with Monotone selected as the Type (which may seem a bit puzzling since you just requested a Duotone). So you will have to select Duotone from the Type pop-up menu.

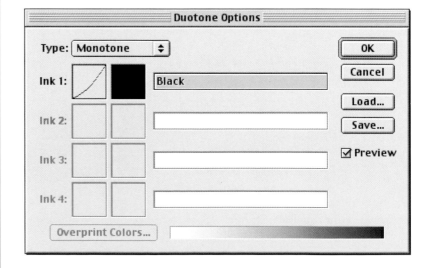

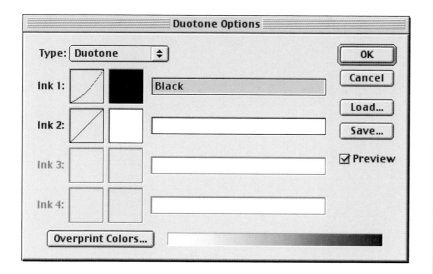

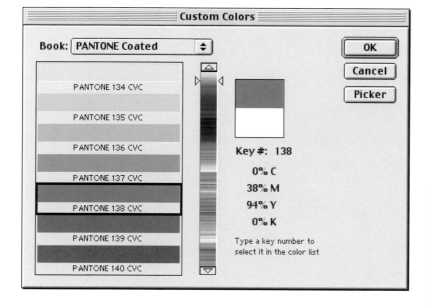

STEP THREE: After you've selected the Type, you have to choose which two inks will comprise your duotone. The box in the first column is a duotone curve, which determines how each ink is applied to the duotone image. (We'll talk about this on the next page. For now, let's focus on picking our two inks.) The box in the second column is the color of the ink for each plate. Ink 1 defaults to Black; ink 2 is generally blank.

STEP FOUR: Click on this blank box to choose the second color. This will bring up Photoshop's Custom Colors selector where you can choose the PANTONE (PMS) color you'd like from the scrolling list. (You can use other color models as well, but it defaults to PANTONE Coated.) A shortcut to selecting PMS numbers is to type in the PMS number on your keyboard. (Note: There is no box to type in the number; just start typing—that's the way it works.)

QUICK TIPS

To create a Duotone, you have to start in Grayscale mode, or the Duotone mode will be grayed out.

STEP FIVE: Now that you've chosen your two colors, you have to decide the balance between them. Will it have more black than your spot color or vice versa? Will there be more black in the shadows and less in the highlights? Yes, you have that kind of control via the Curves setting that is attached to each ink. To view the default curve, click in the first column.

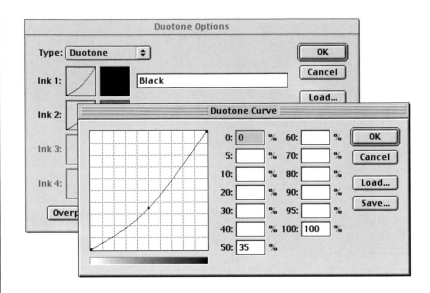

STEP SIX: Don't worry if you're not familiar with Curves, because Adobe anticipated this might be a bit much for first-time duotoners. So they did us all a big favor and created a set of preset duotone curves, along with some of the most popular duotone colors, and believe it or not, they loaded onto your hard drive when you first installed Photoshop. They're just a little bit hard to find (and that's being kind. In reality, they're buried). The great news is you can load these presets into Photoshop's Duotone dialog by clicking on the Load button. But before you do that, click on the Cancel button here in the Duotone Curve dialog box.

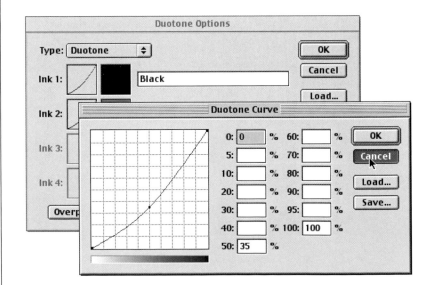

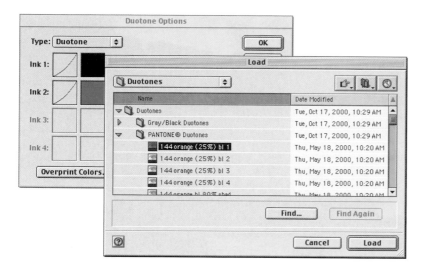

STEP SEVEN: Once you've clicked the Load button in the Duotone Options dialog, the standard Load dialog will appear, and you'll have to navigate your way to your Photoshop application folder (on your hard drive). Look inside the folder called Presets for a folder called Duotones and inside that folder you'll find another folder named Duotones (that's right, inside the Duotones folder there's another folder called Duotones). Inside that folder is yet another folder called PANTONE Duotones (whew!) where Adobe has picked a variety of popular duotone colors and curves for you to use. There are actually four different settings per color, each with a different duotone curve. The first of the four has the most amount of spot color ink, progressing to the least. Click once on the duotone color that you want and then click Load. You will then be returned to the Duotone Options dialog (shown in the next step).

STEP EIGHT: When you load one of Adobe's duotone presets, the curve comes right along with it. You'll see a thumbnail representation of the curve that is applied to Ink 2. As long as you have the Preview turned on (via the checkbox below the Save button) you can preview how the current duotone will look.

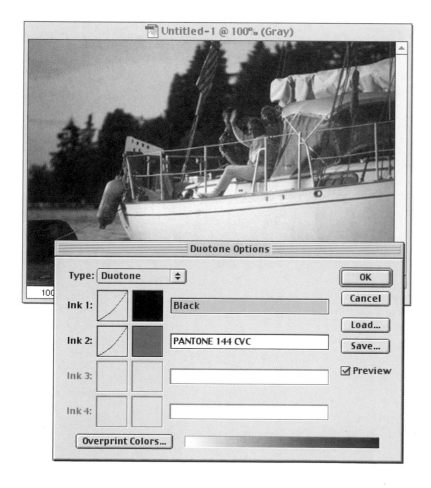

STEP NINE: If you want a different color, just click the Color Swatch in the second column and you can choose a new color from the PANTONE Custom Colors dialog. (Note: choosing a new color doesn't disturb the curve.)

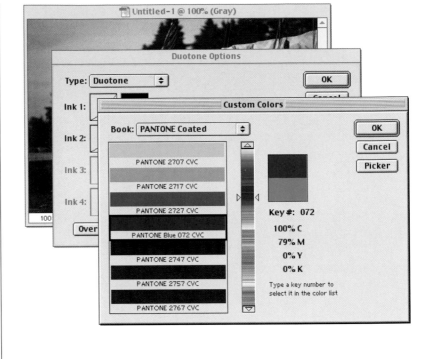

STEP TEN: If you're happy with the way your duotone looks (you're happy with the balance of the two inks), click OK. Now you're ready to save the file, but before you do, you have to make an important change to Photoshop's Page Setup dialog box. To access this area, go under the File menu and choose Page Setup.

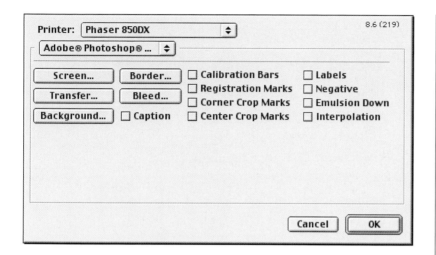

STEP ELEVEN: When this dialog box first appears, click on the Screen button, because we need to have Photoshop assign separate screen angles for our duotone. (With CMYK color images, screen angles are assigned automatically for you, behind the scenes. But with duotones, it's up to you make sure that Photoshop assigns screens.) After you click on the Screen button, a Halftone Screens dialog box will appear.

STEP TWELVE: In this dialog box, Use Printer's Default Screens is checked by default and everything else is grayed out. You have to uncheck this box. When you uncheck it, your ink options will appear. Under Frequency, enter the line screen that this duotone will be printed at. (If you're creating duotones, you're trying to print with just two inks, so chances are you're going to a printing press. We'll assume that's the case here, so we'll use a line screen of 133, a typical line screen for good quality offset presses.) Go under the pop-up menu, choose the second ink and enter the line screen for this ink as well (in this case, 133). And lastly, make sure you check the box marked Use Accurate Screens and hit OK. By doing this, you've assigned a separate screen angle to your second ink, which will keep you from seeing a nasty moiré pattern that would be created if you had printed both plates at the same screen angle.

STEP THIRTEEN: For your duotone to separate and print properly, your file must be saved as an EPS. When you choose EPS as your file format, you'll be presented with the EPS Options dialog box. In this dialog, make sure you select Include Halftone Screen, so the screen angles that you set in the previous step are included with your file. Click OK to save your file and then, as always, print a test to your laser printer or color inkjet printer to make certain that your duotone separates correctly into just two plates—one black and one with your chosen PANTONE color. The final image is shown below right.

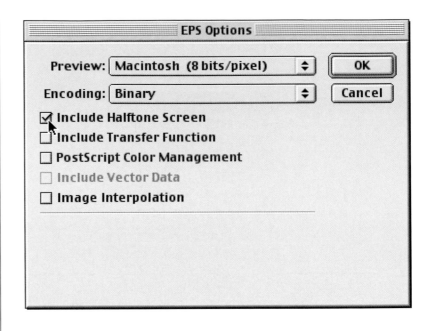

NOTE: There is an area where a lot of people run into problems with duotones—naming of the colors. If you're printing a two-color job and placing this duotone into a page-layout application (such as Adobe InDesign, QuarkXPress, etc.), the name for your spot color in your Photoshop duotone must *exactly* match the name of your spot color in your page-layout application. For example, if you're placing this duotone into a page-layout program where you're using black and PMS 321 CV, then the name of your duotone's Ink 2 in Photoshop must be *exactly the same*: PMS 321 CV. You can't call it "cool blue" or "biz blue." Also, make sure you go to Photoshop's General Preferences (in 5.0/5.5, it's under the File menu; in 6.0 it moved—it's now under the Edit menu) and turn on Short PANTONE Names. This will help Photoshop and your page-layout application match names more easily.

One day, some university will do a study and compile a psychological profile of people who, when asked to

The Thin Red Line

how to clean up line art

provide "camera-ready artwork" of their logo, reach into their wallet and hand you their business card that has their logo at approximately $1/2$" x $1/2$" on textured paper.

When this "camera-ready art" is enlarged to a size you can use for anything other than creating yet another business card, it gets a major case of the "jaggies." There's a special hell for these people.

But this chapter is so much more than that. I'm not quite sure what, but it's got to be more than that, because although it's the shortest chapter in the book, it's not just two pages (which is all it takes to get rid of the jaggies). This poses more questions than it answers (like how, after all these years, do they keep coming up with improved versions of Doritos®. Seriously, how bland were the original Doritos that they keep rolling out more flavorful versions every year? This is the stuff that keeps me up all night). Uh oh, I went "off-topic" again.

Getting Rid of the Jaggies

If you've ever scanned line art, you're probably very familiar with the "jaggies," which are those jaggy, blocky-looking edges that basically make your line art images look just about unusable. Here's how to get rid of those jaggies and smooth out your relationship with your line art.

STEP ONE: Open a line art image that has the jaggies. (Note: This shouldn't be too hard; just ask any of your clients for a logo, and presto!—jaggy line art.)

STEP TWO: Make sure you're in Grayscale mode (you should scan in Grayscale mode, but if you're given line art in Bitmap mode, go under the Image menu, under Mode, and choose Grayscale). Then, go under the Filter menu, under Blur, and choose Gaussian Blur. When the Gaussian Blur dialog box appears, drag the Radius slider to the right until the jaggies disappear, leaving you with a blurry, yet "jaggyless" image.

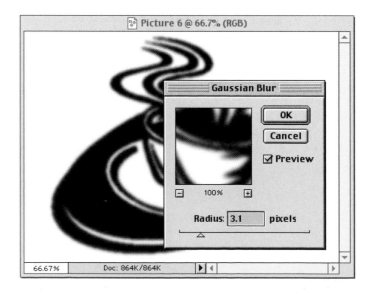

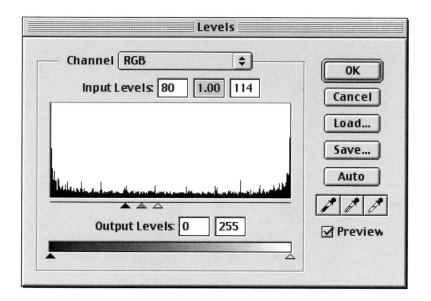

STEP THREE: Go under the Image Menu, under Adjust, and choose Levels. In the Levels dialog box, under the Histogram (the graph), drag the far left shadow slider and the far right highlight slider toward the middle gray midtone slider until all three are almost touching each other (as shown here).

STEP FOUR: When the blurriness is gone, click OK and the jaggies will be gone too. Make sure you read the tip at the bottom of this page for this technique.

QUICK TIPS

This line art technique works well on line "art," but it doesn't work well when the line art contains type. You're better off resetting the type separately, if possible.

Getting Crisper Line Art

This is a combination of two popular techniques that helps you get better, crisper-looking, more detailed line art. We're going to skip the whole debate on resolution, but here's the rub: Many people argue that you should scan line art at the dpi the file will be output (i.e., if you're going to output it at 600 dpi, you should scan it at 600 dpi; if you're outputting at 1,200, scan at 1,200; etc.), but I've always felt life was too short to scan at 1,200 dpi. It's your call.

STEP ONE: Probably the most important Line Art technique is to make sure that you scan the line art in Grayscale mode, rather than in Bitmap (or Line Art) mode in the first place. When you scan in Bitmap mode, you get a simple black-and-white scan (no shades of gray) and therefore, there's really not much to work with in Photoshop—you're already too limited—just black and white lines. However, if you scan in Grayscale, there are a number of options open to you to make the image look better.

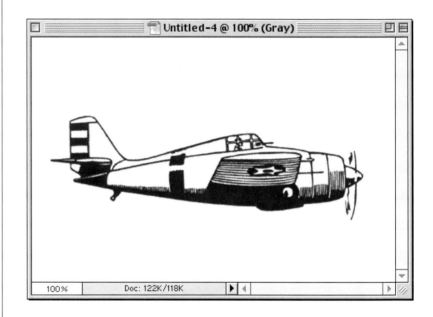

STEP TWO: When you scan line art in Grayscale mode, it may appear a bit soft, but don't let that throw you, because we're going to bring back the sharpness using two Photoshop tools. First is the Unsharp Mask filter. This really helps clean up and define the lines of the line art image, and the more detailed the line art, the more this filter will help. To apply it, go under the Filter menu, under Sharpen, and choose Unsharp Mask. When the dialog box appears, for Amount enter 300%, for Radius enter 1, and for Threshold enter 4 and click OK. In most cases, you can apply this filter more than once (but probably not more than two or three times max).

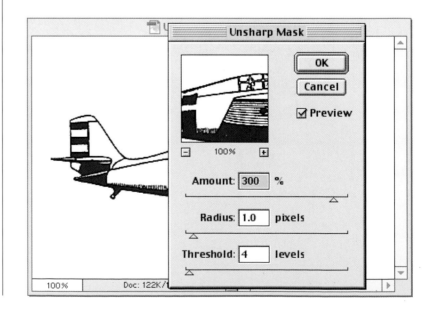

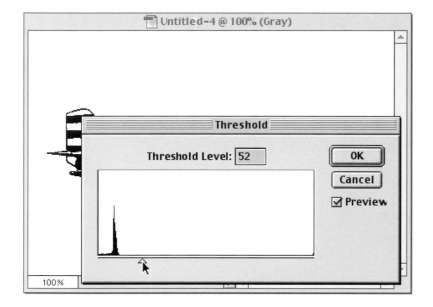

STEP THREE: Once you've evaluated the effects of the sharpening, you then have to remove the "grayness" of the line art so you have crisp black and white lines. To do this, go under the Image menu, under Adjust, and choose Threshold. This dialog lets you determine when the artwork changes from gray to black, giving you a decent level of control over how it will look. When the Threshold dialog box appears, move the slider from the far left to the far right, and you'll get an instant feel for how Threshold affects your line art image. Dragging to the right, the image becomes more detailed (and often messy and busy, so be careful about dragging too far), and dragging to the left cleans the image but drops out detail (so again, be careful). There is no right or wrong amount; you have to use your eye to see what looks best to you.

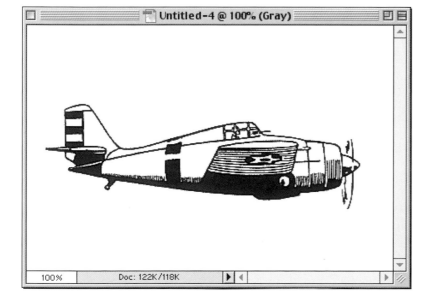

STEP FOUR: Lastly, click OK in the Threshold dialog. Between Sharpening and Threshold, you'll have a better-looking, crisper, more detailed line art image.

Cleaning up Jaggies Quick Tip

This is a tip that I learned early in my Photoshop training, and I really didn't think anyone would care to know it. But I was teaching a Photoshop class at a convention recently and the people attending did a lot of line art cleanup. I casually did this technique as part of another project and it seemed like every hand in the room shot up simultaneously to ask how I did it, so I figured I'd better include it here in the book.

STEP ONE: Open the line art image that needs a cleanup. This particular technique is not a full solution to cleaning up an image—it's just one tip you can use on areas of the image that are supposed to be straight. This works particularly well for cleaning up scanned type, because it contains so many straight lines.

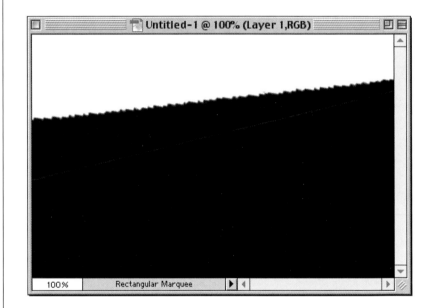

STEP TWO: Press the letter "e" to switch to the Eraser tool. Make sure you have a hard-edged brush tip selected.

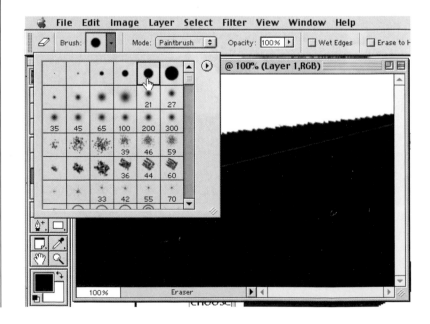

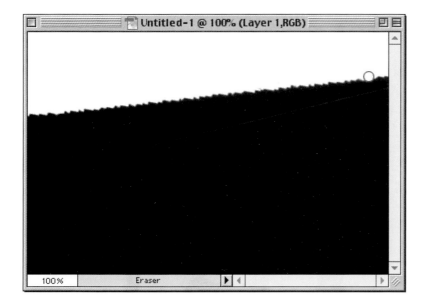

STEP THREE: Find an area of your image that should have a straight smooth line (but instead has a bad case of the jaggies as is shown here). Click once directly on the edge of the jaggy image, making sure your cursor slightly crosses over the edge into the image enough that it erases the jaggies (as shown). Notice how the Eraser cursor digs a little into the edge?

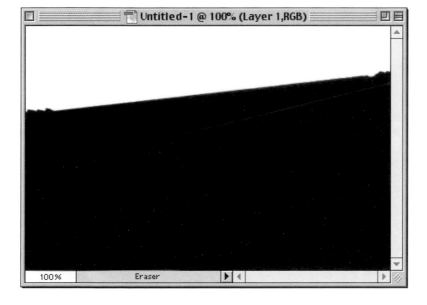

STEP FOUR: Move your cursor (don't click-and-drag) to another point farther along the image. Go as far as you can, but stop before you reach any curved areas. Hold the Shift key and click your cursor once just inside the edge of the jaggy artwork (approximately the same amount as your first click in Step Three). When you do this, it will draw a straight line right along the edge with the Eraser tool, smoothing out the little jaggies and replacing them with a crisp line. You may have to do this numerous times in one product, but this simple trick can really save you a lot of time.

Cut Your Cleanup Time in Half

When you're cleaning up line art, you'll spend a lot of time going to the Toolbox and swapping the foreground (black) and background (white) colors. Of course, you could press the "d" key to set the foreground color to black and then the "x" key every time you need to swap to white, but there's got to be a better way, right? Right.

STEP ONE: Open the line art image that you want to clean up. Press the "z" key to switch to the Zoom tool, and then click the tool twice within your image area to zoom in. Press Shift-B until the Pencil tool appears in the Toolbox (it lives behind the Paintbrush tool).

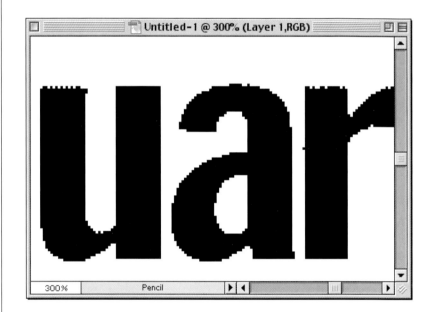

STEP TWO: In the Options Bar there's an option called Auto Erase. Turn this option on and your trips to the Toolbox or to the "d" and "x" keys are over. That's because, thankfully, Auto Erase does nothing like what it sounds. Now when you click in an area that is white, your Pencil tool will paint black. When you click in an area that's black, it will automatically paint in white. Anytime you want to change colors, just click the mouse again and start painting. This can cut your line art cleanup time in half. You can also hold the Shift key to draw straight lines along the letters, cutting even more cleanup time.

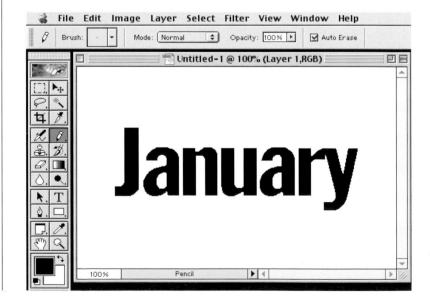

Turning Photos into Line Art

Here's a quick technique using Photoshop's own filters to turn any photograph into line art. There are also third-party plug-ins available that do an amazing job of converting photos into detailed *Wall Street Journal*-style line art drawings. The most notable of these is Andromeda's excellent Cutline Filter™ plug-in. You can download a demo tryout version (for Mac and PC) from www.andromeda.com.

STEP ONE: Open the photograph that you want to convert into line art.

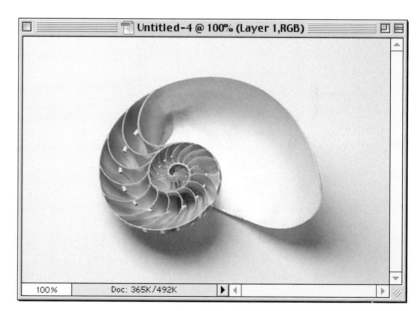

STEP TWO: Go under the Filter menu, under Stylize, and choose Find Edges, and Photoshop will trace the edges of the image for you. (Note: The more clearly defined the edges are, the better job Find Edges will do.)

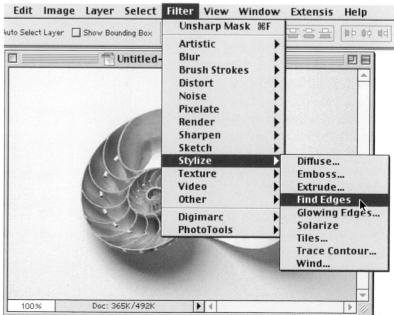

STEP THREE: The Find Edges filter unfortunately introduces some colors to the image that have to be removed for it to look like line art, so you'll have to remove them. Luckily, all you have to do is press Shift-Command-U (PC: Shift-Control-U) to Desaturate the image and remove all the color.

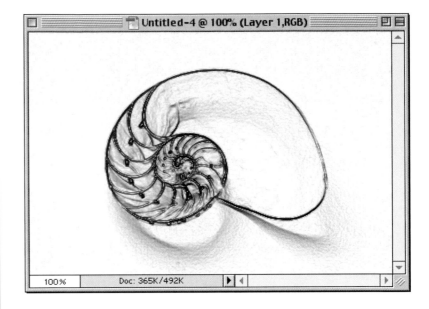

STEP FOUR: Besides the color intrusion (that we dealt with in the previous step), the Find Edges filter often creates a cluttered look by leaving thin lines and other artifacts throughout the image. To remove that cluttered look, press Command-L (PC: Control-L) to bring up the Levels dialog box. When the dialog box appears, grab the top right Input Levels slider (the white one) and drag it to the left. As you do this, you'll see some of those faint lines disappear and you'll see areas that were gray and messy start to become white. When the image looks like a nice line art drawing click OK.

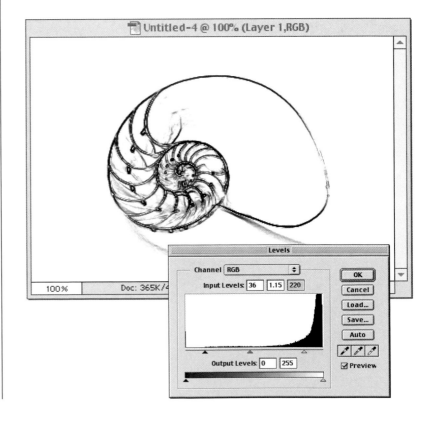

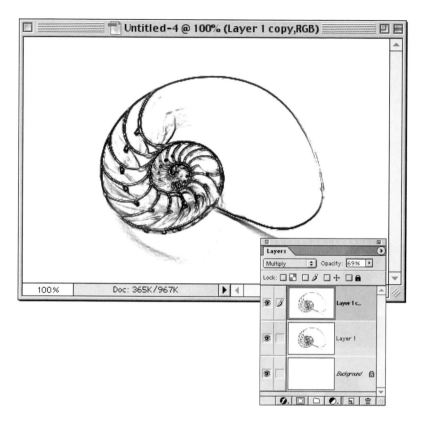

STEP FIVE: There's a good chance that by lightening the image with Levels (in the previous step) the lines that remain may be a bit light (or shall we say, a bit gray). To thicken and darken these lines, make a duplicate of this layer by dragging it to the New Layer icon at the bottom of the Layers palette. Then, change the blend mode of this layer from Normal to Multiply. This thickens and darkens the outlines of your line art.

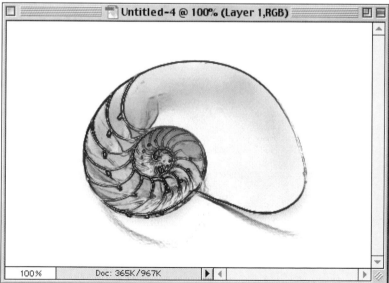

STEP SIX: This step is optional, but if you decide you want to colorize your line art, you can cheat and use the History Brush to paint back in a faint shade of the original image. Here's how: First, click on your line art layer (your original line art layer, not the one on top that's set to Multiply). Then, press the "y" key to switch to the History Brush. In the Options Bar, lower the Opacity to around 40%, choose a soft-edged brush, and start painting back in your original image. Don't paint too many strokes or it will start to look like a photograph again.

CHAPTER nine

There has to be a chapter in every Photoshop book where the author can put the techniques that don't really fit

Dirty Work

other retouching dirty tricks

anywhere else. Well, guess what? This is that chapter. It's a catchall for some pretty cool tips that just need a good home (all their shots are up to date, and they're totally housebroken).

We're talking photographic effects, blur effects, brush techniques… you know—stuff that sounds important, and better yet, looks totally legitimate on client invoices. I figure it this way, if you learn nothing but the techniques included in this one chapter, you can not only earn the money back you paid for this book but you can also earn enough to buy eight or nine more copies of this book to give as gifts to friends, co-workers, or even relatives. The real measure of your success as a retoucher is how many more copies of this book you buy and distribute to other people. Are you buying into this? You are? See, this is why I love this whole "book-writing" thing.

Bringing Back Lost Color in the Shadows

This is a quick trick you can use to bring back color and detail in the shadow areas of your image. This works particularly well in landscapes where you want to accentuate color in the shadow areas and make the darker areas of your image more vibrant.

STEP ONE: Open an image that has shadow areas in which you want to bring out the color.

STEP TWO: Go under the Select menu and choose Color Range. From the Select pop-up menu at the top of the dialog box, choose Shadows. Just click OK, and Color Range will automatically select all the shadow areas within your image.

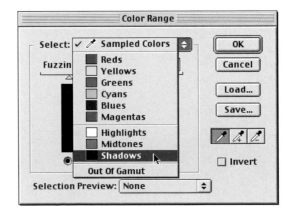

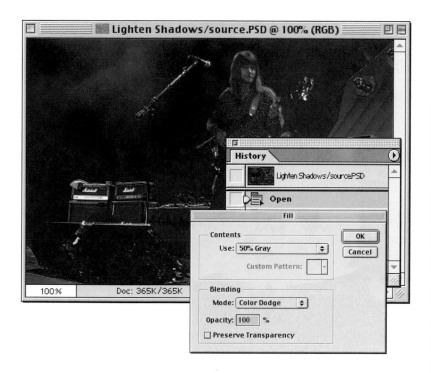

STEP THREE: While the selection is in place, go under the Edit menu and choose Fill. When the Fill dialog box appears, in the Use pop-up menu in the Contents section, choose 50% Gray. In the Blending section, change the Mode from Normal to Color Dodge. Leave the Opacity at 100%, then click OK. Repeat this same Fill process again for a total of two times. Your image will probably appear very oversaturated, but don't let that throw you. Press Command-D (PC: Control-D) to Deselect.

STEP FOUR: Go under the Window menu and choose Show History. In the History palette, click on the Open state. Your image will return to the way it looked when you first opened it. The other states will still be listed in the palette, but they'll be grayed out. Click once in the first column beside the Fill state. By doing this, you're telling Photoshop that you want to paint from how the image looked after you performed the Fill.

QUICK TIPS

Another way to load the shadow areas of your image as a feathered selection is to press Option-Command-~ (PC: Alt-Control-~).

STEP FIVE: Press the "y" key to switch to the History Brush. In the Options Bar, lower the Opacity for this tool to 50%. Choose a soft-edged brush and start painting over the shadow areas to accentuate the color. In the image at right, I painted over the vocal monitors at the bottom left of the image.

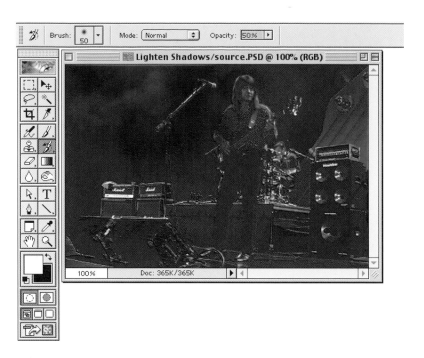

STEP SIX: Continue painting until the shadows have additional detail and vibrancy. If you need more vibrancy, release the mouse button and then click and paint over the same areas again. In the image shown here, I painted over the monitors (as I mentioned earlier), the amps on both sides of the stage, the bass he's holding, his pants, and the skirt on the drum riser. Notice the additional detail and color in those areas. Here you can see the original image (on top) and the retouched image (on bottom).

Original image without enhanced shadow areas

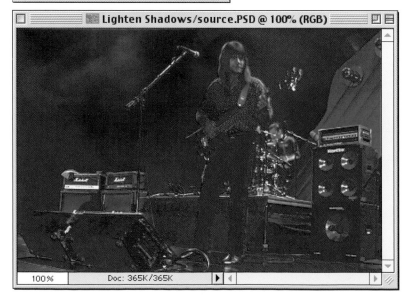

Instant Polaroid Effect

This is a technique that I've been doing in one of my live Photoshop sessions for the past few years. I got the idea from a Saturn® auto ad that used what looked like a Polaroid® image of one of their customers, but upon closer inspection, I realized they had actually created the whole thing in Photoshop.

STEP ONE: Open the photo you want to turn into a Polaroid. Press Command-A (PC: Control-A) to select the entire image. Press Shift-Command-J (PC: Shift-Control-J) to put the image onto its own separate layer. Then go under the Image menu and choose Canvas Size. When the Canvas Size dialog box appears, increase the values in the Width and Height boxes to add extra white canvas space on all sides of your image (as shown here).

STEP TWO: Create a new blank layer by clicking on the New Layer icon at the bottom of the Layers palette. Press the "m" key to switch to the Rectangular Marquee tool and draw a selection that is about 1/2" larger than your image on the top and sides, and about 1" below the bottom (this will act as the border for your Polaroid image). Choose a very light gray as your foreground color, then fill your selection with light gray by pressing Option-Delete (PC: Alt-Backspace).

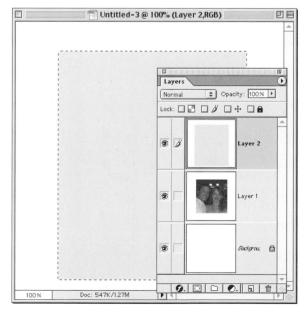

STEP THREE: Deselect by pressing Command-D (PC: Control-D). Then, in the Layers palette, drag this gray layer behind your image layer (as shown). Click on your top layer (your image layer) then press Command-E (PC: Control-E) to merge your top layer with the gray layer below it.

STEP FOUR: Make a copy of this merged layer by dragging it to the New Layer icon at the bottom of the Layers palette. Press the "d" key to set your foreground color to black. Then, press Shift-Option-Delete (PC: Shift-Alt-Backspace) to fill your merged layer with black.

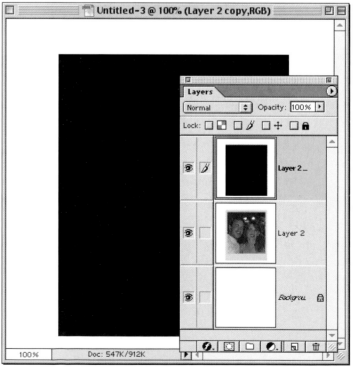

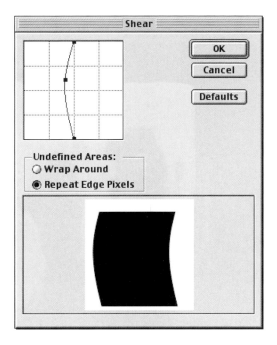

STEP FIVE: Go under the Filter menu, under Distort, and choose Shear. When the Shear dialog box appears, click on the line just above the center of the grid in the dialog box. This adds a center point to the grid. Click-and-drag this point to the left (as shown here). The bottom of the dialog box shows a preview of how your shear will look. When it looks like the preview shown at left, click OK.

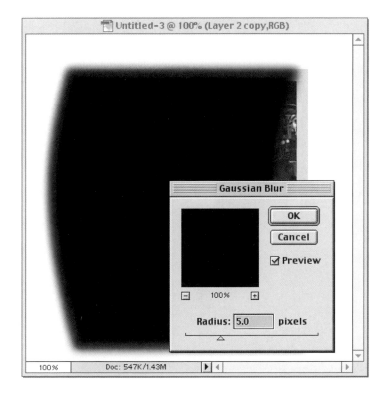

STEP SIX: Drag this black, sheared layer behind your image layer. Go under the Filter menu, under Blur, and choose Gaussian Blur. Enter a Radius of 5 and click OK (enter a Radius of 11 for high-res, 300-ppi images).

STEP SEVEN: Press the "v" key to switch to the Move tool. Then drag this black, sheared layer to the right until the corners peak out, giving the impression that the shadow is bent (as shown).

STEP EIGHT: The left side of the shadow will probably be sticking out from behind the left side of your image, so you'll need to tuck it in a bit. Press Command-T (PC: Control-T) to bring up Free Transform. Grab the left center control point of the bounding box and drag inward to safely hide the left side of the shadow behind the image. Press Return (PC: Enter) when the left side shadow is hidden. Now, in the Layers palette, lower the Opacity of this layer to 70%.

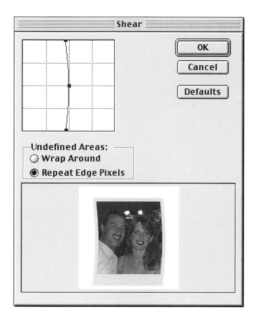

STEP NINE: Now that your shadow is bent, we have to bend the image itself. First, in the Layers palette, click on your image layer to make it active. Then, go under the Filter menu, under Distort, and choose Shear. When the Shear dialog appears, it will still have the last settings you applied in the grid. Click-and-drag the center point back to the center (making the image flat). Now, click-and-drag the top and bottom points (on the grid line) to the left, to bend the top and bottom edges of the image. Click OK.

STEP TEN: To complete the effect, in the Layers palette, click in the first column next to the sheared shadow layer to link it temporarily with the image layer. Now, press Command-T (PC: Control-T) to bring up Free Transform. Move your cursor outside the Free Transform bounding box and click-and-drag in a circular motion to rotate the image. When the rotation looks good to you, press Return (PC: Enter).

Glamour Photo Effect

This simple Photoshop technique gives the effect of using a camera with a soft focus filter applied. Back in the old days (when dinosaurs roamed the earth) some glamour photographers would actually apply a tiny bit of Vaseline® to their lens to give a soft dreamy effect. You can also replicate this effect by applying a tiny bit of Vaseline to your monitor—but I wouldn't suggest it.

STEP ONE: Open an image that you want to give an overall soft, dreamy look.

STEP TWO: In the Layers palette, click-and-drag the Background layer to the New Layer icon at the bottom of the Layers palette. This makes a duplicate of the Background layer.

STEP THREE: Go under the Filter menu, under Blur, and choose Gaussian Blur. For low-res, 72-ppi images, enter a Radius of 4 (for high-res images, try 8 to 10).

STEP FOUR: In the Layers palette, change the layer's blend mode from Normal to Lighten to create the effect. If the effect is too soft and blurry, decrease the Opacity setting for this layer until it's just the way you like it.

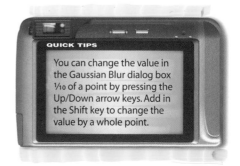

QUICK TIPS

You can change the value in the Gaussian Blur dialog box ¹/₁₀ of a point by pressing the Up/Down arrow keys. Add in the Shift key to change the value by a whole point.

Adding Motion Effects to Backgrounds

Adding motion effects to a background used to be a tedious task, requiring intricate selections and masking. That's because it would affect the foreground objects as well as the background. But since Adobe introduced the History feature back in Photoshop 5.0, adding a motion effect to the background has now become a very simple procedure.

STEP ONE: Open an image that has a background that you want to apply a motion effect to.

STEP TWO: Go under the Filter menu, under Blur, and choose Motion Blur. When the Motion Blur dialog box appears, choose which direction you want the blur to go, using the Angle control. Use the Distance slider to add the desired amount of Motion Blur. Applying this blur will affect the entire image, but don't worry about that just yet. If the amount of blur on the background looks right to you, click OK.

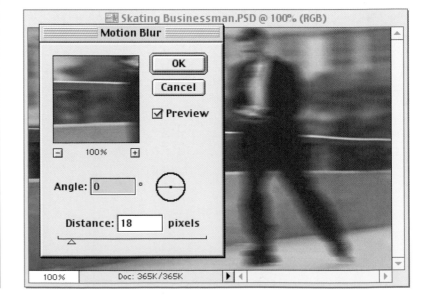

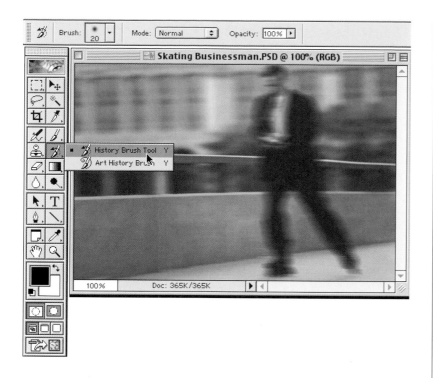

STEP THREE: Press the letter "y" to switch to the History Brush. The History Brush is kind of like having an undo on a brush. When you paint with it using its default settings, it automatically paints back to what the image looked like when you first opened it.

STEP FOUR: Choose a soft-edged brush and paint over the areas that you don't want to be affected by the Motion Blur to complete the effect.

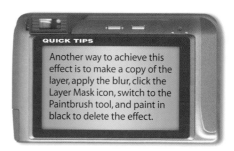

QUICK TIPS

Another way to achieve this effect is to make a copy of the layer, apply the blur, click the Layer Mask icon, switch to the Paintbrush tool, and paint in black to delete the effect.

Background Vignette Effect

In the next chapter of the book, we show you how to create the classic, soft-edged vignette effect, but here we're showing a much cooler trick. Rather than removing the edges of the background, we're going to keep it and blur it. We'll then use a Layer Mask to make the transition between the blurred background and the focal point of the image very smooth.

STEP ONE: Open an image where you want to apply the background vignette effect. (That's my son Jordan getting his first stripe on his belt in Karate. I just love that little guy!)

STEP TWO: In the Layers palette, make a copy of your Background layer by dragging it to the New Layer icon at the bottom of the palette. Next, go under the Filter menu, under Blur, and choose Gaussian Blur. When the dialog box appears, enter the amount of blur you'd like to apply to the background (I used a Radius of 10.4 in this example), then click OK.

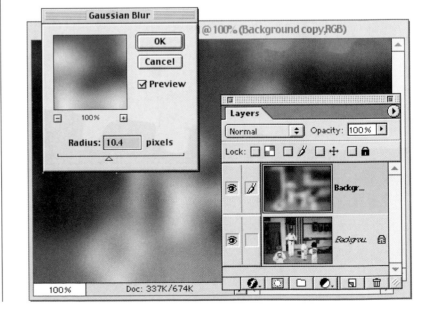

STEP THREE: Make another copy of your Background layer by dragging it to the New Layer icon at the bottom of the Layers palette. When the copied layer appears in the palette, click on it and drag it to the top of the layers stack. The stacking order from top to bottom should now be: Clean layer on top, blurry layer in the middle, original Background layer on the bottom.

STEP FOUR: Now, using a selection tool of your choice, draw a very loose selection around the part of the image you want to focus attention on. In this instance, I put a circular selection on the focal point using the Elliptical Marquee selection tool, but you can use any tool you like, including the Lasso tool.

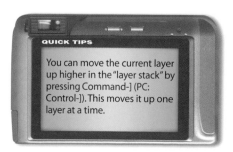

QUICK TIPS

You can move the current layer up higher in the "layer stack" by pressing Command-] (PC: Control-]). This moves it up one layer at a time.

STEP FIVE: Go under the Select menu and choose Feather. When the Feather Selection dialog box appears, enter 25 for your Feather Radius if you're using a low-res image (use 50 for high-res images), and click OK.

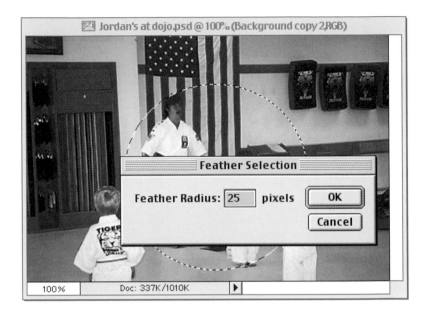

STEP SIX: To complete the effect, go to the Layers palette and click on the Layer Mask icon at the bottom of the Layers palette (it's the second icon from the left), and you'll see the final effect (shown here).

Adding Starbursts

This is a quick technique for creating little starbursts on your image. This is traditionally added to images when you want to have a little twinkle, or to draw attention to certain areas of the image.

STEP ONE: Open an image that you want to add starbursts to. (No, that's not my car. Get all of your friends to buy this book, then… maybe. Of course, you'd have to have an awful lot of friends.)

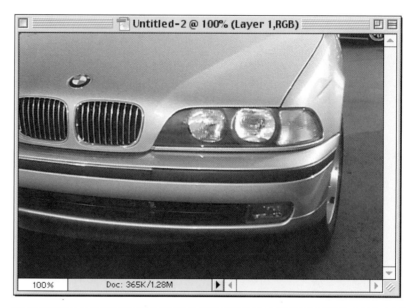

STEP TWO: Press the "j" key to switch to the Airbrush tool. Up in the Options Bar, lower the Pressure setting to 25%. Then open the Brushes pop-down menu by clicking on the down-facing triangle to the right of the thumbnail of the currently selected brush tip. When the Brushes pop-down menu appears, click on the right-facing triangle to reveal a pop-down menu. At the bottom of the menu are sets of brushes you can load into the Brushes menu. Choose Assorted Brushes from the list. From the dialog box that appears, choose Append to add these brushes to your palette without replacing the default set of brushes.

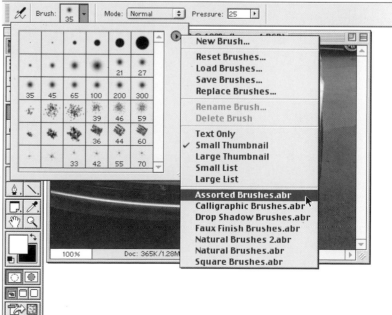

STEP THREE: In the Brushes pop-down menu, scroll down until you reach the 48-pixel brush that looks like an "X" (as shown here). Click on that brush to select it. Press "d" then "x" to set your foreground color to white.

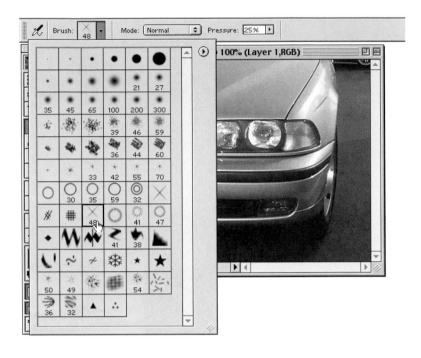

STEP FOUR: Once the brush is selected, click-and-hold the brush for just a moment over the areas where you want to add the starbursts. In this example, I applied two starbursts—one on the BMW® emblem and one on the bumper.

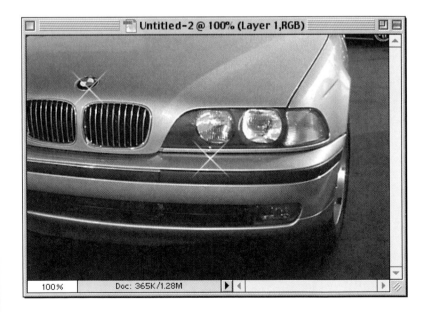

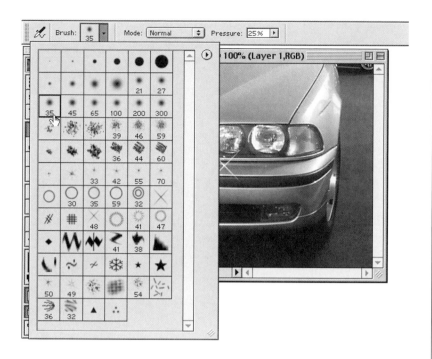

STEP FIVE: Go back to the Brushes pop-down menu again, but this time choose a smaller, soft-edged brush from the default set of brushes. (In this example, I chose a 35-pixel, soft-edged brush.)

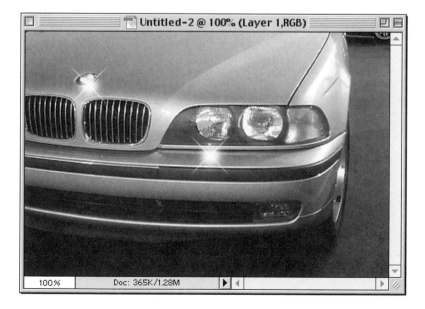

STEP SIX: To complete the effect, click the Airbrush tool once in the center of each starburst to soften the center, making the effect look more realistic.

QUICK TIPS

To get the Airbrush tool to act more like a real airbrush, lower the Opacity to 70%, change the blend mode to Multiply, and then apply your layers of paint.

Quick Color Change for an Object

This is a very quick way to change the color of a particular object within your image. The method we're showing here is based on making a selection of the area you want to change and recoloring it using Photoshop's Hue/Saturation command.

STEP ONE: Open an image that has an object the color of which you want to change. In this case, our fictitious client has asked us to change the color of the helmet from red to blue.

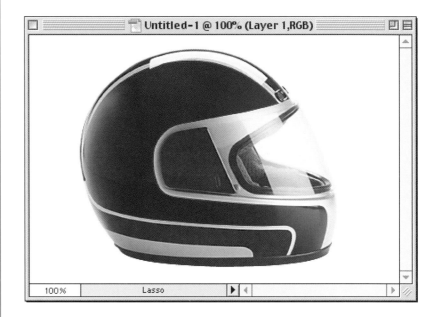

STEP TWO: Use the Magic Wand tool (press the "w" key) to help you select the red areas of the helmet . Start by clicking once within a red portion, then hold the Shift key and continue clicking in the unselected red areas until they are all selected. (Note: After I selected the helmet, I zoomed in on the image and noticed that I had missed a few stray red pixels along the edge, so I went under the Select menu and chose Similar. This automatically selects any other pixels in the image that share the same color as the pixels that are already selected, so basically it selected the rest of the red pixels for me.)

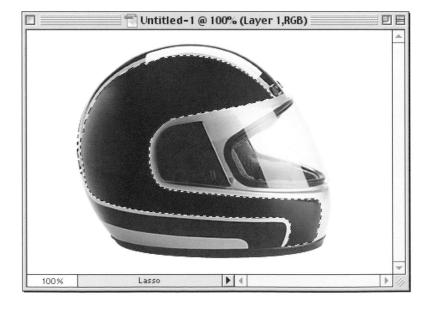

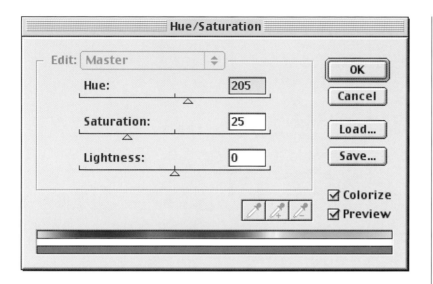

STEP THREE: Go under the Image menu, under Adjust, and choose Hue/Saturation. When the dialog box appears, look in the bottom right-hand corner and you'll find a checkbox for Colorize. Turn it on, and then drag the Hue slider to the right to find the shade of blue you're looking for. In this example, I used a value of 205. When it looks about right, click OK.

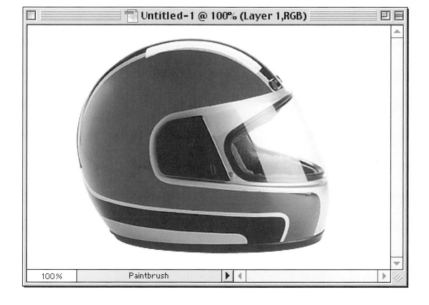

STEP FOUR: Now that you've completed the color change, press Command-D (PC: Control-D) to Deselect and reveal your completed color retouch.

QUICK TIPS

You can colorize black and white images by converting to RGB mode, then choose a foreground color, and paint with the Paintbrush tool with its Blend mode set to Color.

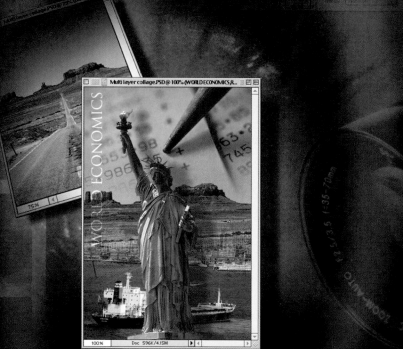

Since this is a retouching book, we're going to look at collaging photos from a different angle. Start by

Come Together
photo-collaging techniques

tilting the book about 45° to the left and see if that makes a difference. (OK, that was pretty lame, but I'm stalling for time.)

Collaging is about photos and images coming together in perfect harmony. Actually, I'd like to teach the world to sing in perfect harmony. But in the meantime, we're going to look at some techniques for collaging, including layer masks, vignettes (which are popular for vintage retouching), and getting rid of the fringe pixels that sometimes appear on the edges of objects that you're compositing on a background (whatever that means).

Layer Masks for Collaging

This is my absolute favorite technique for collaging, because it's so flexible and so much fun. The technique actually requires only three clicks: one on the Layer Mask icon, one to get the Gradient tool, and one just before you drag the Gradient tool through your image.

STEP ONE: Open a base image you want to use in your collage.

STEP TWO: Open the second image you want to use in your collage. Press the "v" key to switch to the Move tool, and click-and-drag this image into the first document that you opened. Make sure the images overlap each other.

STEP THREE: To blend the two images together, click on the Layer Mask icon at the bottom of the Layers palette (it's the second one from the left). Then press the letter "g" to switch to the Gradient tool. Make sure the Gradient chosen is the default Foreground to Background gradient by clicking on the down-facing arrow next to the gradient sample in the Options Bar. Press the "d" key to set your foreground color to black and the background color to white. Drag the Gradient tool through your image and the two images will blend. (Note: If the blend goes in the wrong direction, just try dragging again in the opposite direction.)

STEP FOUR: Next, open a third image and use the Move tool to drag this image on top of your existing collage.

QUICK TIPS

When using Layer Masks for collaging, painting on the layer in black erases the image. Painting in white paints it back in. Use a large, soft-edged brush for smoother transitions.

STEP FIVE: Now, we'll apply a Layer Mask to this new layer as well. Use the same three-step process: (1) click on the Layer Mask icon, (2) press the letter "g" to switch to the Gradient tool, and then (3) drag the Gradient tool through your image to make it blend or appear to fade out (as shown here).

STEP SIX: To finish off this collage, I opened an image of the Statue of Liberty and dragged it on top of the other images to bring the whole collage together and act as a focal point. I made a copy of the statue layer, filled it with black, ran a 4-pixel Gaussian Blur, and dragged it behind the Statue of Liberty layer to create a drop shadow. I also added some type with the Type tool and changed the blend mode (in the Layers palette) of the Type layer from Normal to Overlay to help the type blend into the background.

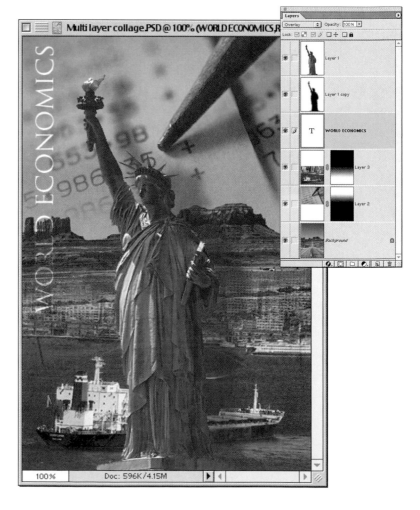

Hiding Edge Pixels when Collaging

If you're selecting images from one document and dragging (or pasting) them into another, you're bound to wind up with some edge pixels. You know, those nasty, white little pixels along the edge (they're not always white—it depends on which color the background was in the original image, but they're almost always there).

STEP ONE: Open a background image that you want to use for the collage. Open a second image that has an object in it that you want to drag into the background image. Use your favorite selection tool (Lasso, Magic Wand, etc.) to select your object. Press the "v" key to switch to the Move tool, then click-and-drag the object to the background image. Look for edge pixels around the object.

STEP TWO: Go under the Layer menu, under Matting, and choose Defringe.

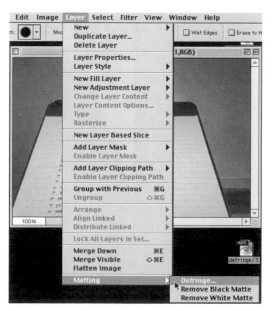

STEP THREE: When the Defringe dialog box appears, start by trying the default setting of one pixel and click OK (this will usually do the trick).

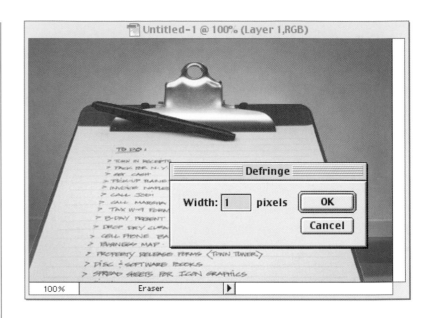

STEP FOUR: When you click OK on Defringe, Photoshop replaces the old, edge pixels with a new, edge pixel that is a combination of the foreground image and the background image behind it. If you choose a 1-pixel Defringe, it only affects 1 pixel deep. If you choose a higher number, if affects a deeper number of pixels. The default setting of 1 will usually do the trick.

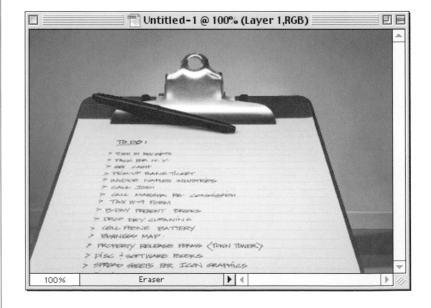

QUICK TIPS

Another edge-smoothing trick is to draw a Path (with the Pen tool) along the edge, choose Stroke Path from the Paths palette's menu, and choose the Smudge tool from the dialog.

Adding Objects to an Existing Image

This is a surprisingly common request—adding an object to an existing image. In this instance, we're going to replace the laptop in the man's hands with a different object with a little help from Photoshop's Layer Mask.

STEP ONE: Open an image that you want to add an object to.

STEP TWO: Open the image of the object you want to add to your existing image. Use the selection tool of your choice to select this object. (When an object is on a white background, like the image shown at right, you can use the Magic Wand tool. Just click once on the white background to select it, then go under the Select menu and chose Inverse, which will inverse the selection, giving you a selection of the object, rather than the background.)

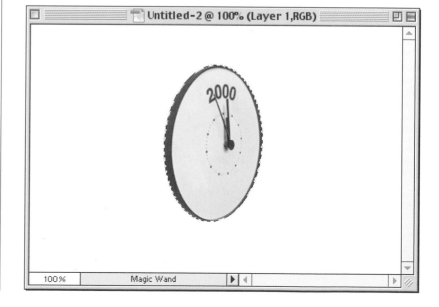

STEP THREE: Press the "v" key to switch to the Move tool. Click on your selected object and drag it into the other image. Use the Move tool to position the object where you want it to appear within your image.

STEP FOUR: In the Layers palette, lower the opacity of this layer so you can see the image behind it. In the example shown here, I lowered Opacity to 63%.

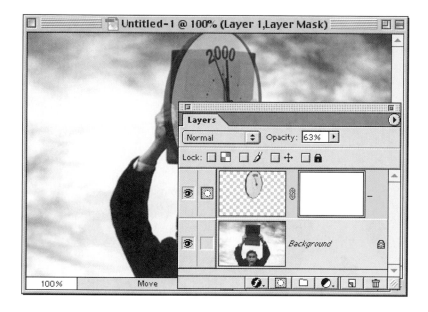

STEP FIVE: We're going to have to remove the area of the object that is covering the man's fingers so it will appear that he's holding the object. To do this, you'll use a Layer Mask, so click on the Layer Mask icon at the bottom of the Layers palette (it's the second icon from the left).

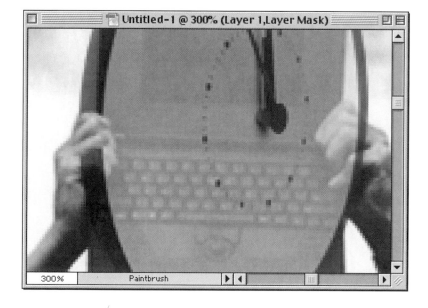

STEP SIX: Press the "z" key to switch to the Zoom tool, and click twice within your image to zoom in on the areas where the man's fingers are. Press the "x" key until your foreground color is set to black. Press the letter "b" to switch to the Paintbrush tool. Choose a small, hard-edged brush, about the size of the fingers or just slightly smaller, and start painting over the fingers. Because you lowered the opacity of the object layer, you'll be able to see where the fingers are, and because you're painting on the Layer Mask in black, it just paints away the object (in this case a clock) revealing the fingers beneath. If you accidentally erase too much, press the letter "x" to switch to white and paint the clock back in. That's the beauty of the Layer Mask.

STEP SEVEN: Continue painting over the fingers until they're visible and the clock areas covering them have been masked away.

STEP EIGHT: In the Layers palette, raise the opacity of the object (clock) layer back to 100%. There's still work to be done, because the corners of the computer the man was holding are still peaking out from behind the clock.

STEP NINE: In the Layers palette, click on the Background layer to make it active. Press the "s" key to switch to the Rubber Stamp tool. Sample an area to either the left or right of each corner, then paint (clone) over the corners on the top and bottom of the image.

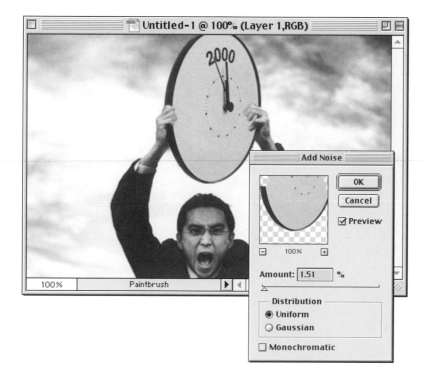

STEP TEN: At this point he's holding the object, but it still looks like the object was "stuck there," because it's too crisp and bright to blend in with the rest of the image. To make it look more realistic, go under the Image menu, under Adjust, and choose Levels. When the dialog box appears, move the lower right Output Levels slider to the left a little to darken the clock layer until it better matches the overall tone of the image. Lastly, go under the Filter menu, under Noise, and choose Add Noise. When the dialog box appears, for Amount choose 1.5% (for high-res images use 3%), leave the Distribution set to Uniform, and click OK to apply a little bit of grain to the image. This will also help sell the effect that the object was part of the original image.

Feathering Tutorial

Feathering is used to soften the edges of a selection, and is particularly helpful in photo retouching. This particular tutorial is designed to show you how critical adding a small amount of feathering can be, and after completing this tutorial, you'll have a good idea of how, when, and why feathering should be applied.

STEP ONE: Open an image that has an area that is washed-out and needs to be adjusted to match the rest of the image. Make a duplicate of this image by going under the Image menu and choosing Duplicate. This will open up another document window with a copy of the image.

STEP TWO: In this duplicate of your original, press the "L" key to switch to the Lasso tool, and draw a selection around the area that needs to be adjusted.

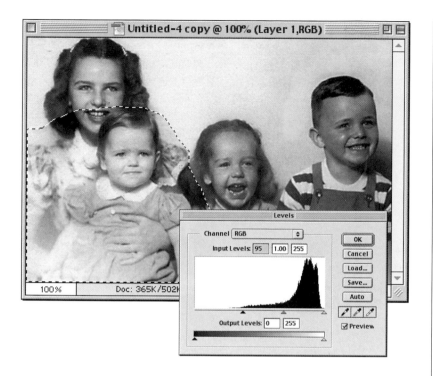

STEP THREE: Go under the Image menu, under Adjust, and choose Levels. In the Levels dialog box, under the Histogram (the graph that looks like a mountain range), move the left shadow Input Levels slider (the black one on the far left) to the right until the overall tone matches the rest of the image. In some cases, you'll have to move both the shadow slider and the midtone slider to the right until the tone matches.

STEP FOUR: Press Command-D (PC: Control-D) to deselect. Now, take a look at the area you've selected and see how harsh the edges are and how obvious your tonal retouch appears. That's because there's not a smooth transition between your retouched area and the rest of the image—the kind of smoothing feathering creates. Up to this point, you've been working on a duplicate of your original image, so now switch back to your original image.

QUICK TIPS

Here's a trick that allows you to see the effects of feathering: Make your selection, switch to Quick Mask mode ("q"), apply a Gaussian Blur, and you can see how soft your edges will be.

STEP FIVE: Using the selection tool you used earlier, reselect the same area you selected previously.

STEP SIX: After your selection is in place, go under the Select menu and choose Feather. In the Feather Selection dialog box, enter a Feather Radius setting of 5 (try 8 or 9 for high-res images).

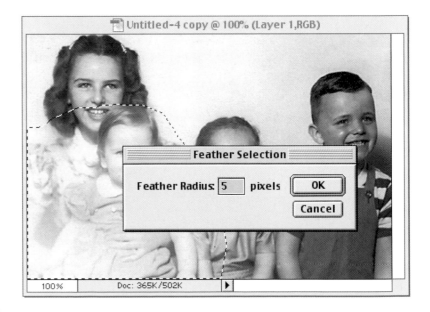

STEP SEVEN: Go under the Image Menu, under Adjust, and choose Levels. Make the same adjustments you made earlier with the shadow and midtone sliders.

STEP EIGHT: Deselect by pressing Command-D (PC: Control-D) and look at the image. Notice how the transition between your selected area and the rest of the image is now very smooth, and you don't see the hard edge where your selection was. Arrange your images on screen so you can see both your original document and the duplicate image. Looking at the difference, you should now be able to understand the value of feathering and how it can help in your retouching tasks.

Vignette Effect

This technique is used for adding a soft-edged effect around your image, adding a dreamy look to the overall image. Vignettes are popular with wedding photographers and in photos of children. It's also often used for adding a bit of elegance to images in advertising of jewelry, fine homes, etc. You can also use it to cheat in retouching when you have an image whose subject looks fine, but the background is trashed. Hey, I said it was cheating.

STEP ONE: Open an image that you want to add the vignette effect to.

STEP TWO: Press Shift-M until the Elliptical Marquee tool appears at the top of the Toolbox. Draw a tall oval selection around the area you want to keep. Because the vignette effect will add a soft border, you should make your selection a little larger than the area you want to keep.

STEP THREE: To soften the edges, go under the Select menu and choose Feather (or use the keyboard shortcut Option-Command-D [PC: Alt-Control-D]). When the Feather dialog box appears, you'll be prompted to enter a Feather Radius. The higher the number you choose, the softer (and wider) your edge will be. (For this example, on a low-res, 72-ppi image, I used 10 pixels.) Choose your Feather Radius and then click OK. You won't see any change in your image at this point.

STEP FOUR: Go under the Select menu and choose Inverse (this changes the selection from what's inside the oval to the background area). Press Delete (PC: Backspace) to remove the background, creating a soft-edged oval around your image, as shown here. The next step looks at a potential problem that may occur when collaging images using vignettes.

STEP FIVE: What happens if you want to put this vignette over a different background, perhaps for a collaging technique? That requires a slight change in the technique, because if you use it the way it is now, this is what you'll get—a solid white background around your vignette, which makes for a pretty lame-looking collage. Here's how to get around that: Remember back in Step Four, we had you inverse your selection and then hit Delete? Don't do that. Skip Step Four, and instead, after you apply the feather, go under the Edit menu and choose Copy.

STEP SIX: Now, move to the background image you want to use, go under the Edit menu, and choose Paste, and the vignette will paste in and blend smoothly with your image *without* the annoying white background.

CHAPTER ELEVEN

What happens if a client asks you to set up a product shot or an executive portrait and although you have

Studio 54

studio and advertising effects

a digital camera, you don't have your own studio? What do you do? It's simple—you break into somebody else's studio late at night. The guard dog probably won't be much of a problem, but the studio owner and his son... well, that's an entirely different story. You'll have to beat them to death with their own shoes. (Note to Editor: I wonder if anyone will get that obscure Wayne's World 2 reference? Nah, probably not. Let's pull it before we go to press.)

This chapter looks at how to replicate traditional studio effects, and some of the more popular commercial advertising techniques.

Setting up a Studio Product Shot

In this example, we're going to make it look like we went into a studio and set up a product shot. We're starting with a stock photo of a flat backdrop like you might see in a traditional studio, but we're going to use Photoshop to make it look like we set up an actual product photo shoot.

STEP ONE: Open an image of a backdrop. (Note: This technique will work with most backgrounds that have some sort of texture to them. Without the texture, you won't be able to see the "bend" in the background where it meets the floor, therefore, killing the whole effect.)

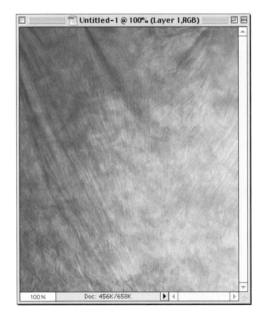

STEP TWO: Press the "m" key to switch to the Rectangular Marquee tool, and draw a rectangular selection around the entire bottom third of your background (as shown here).

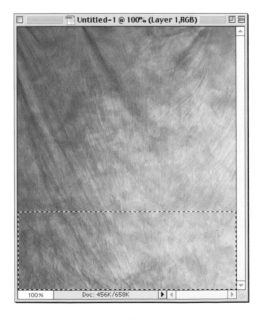

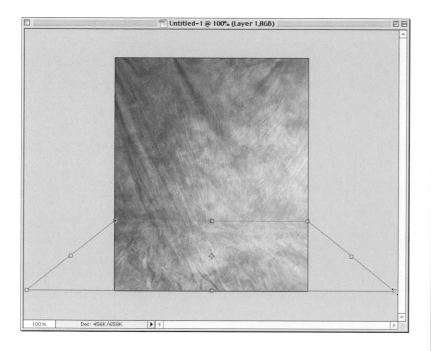

STEP THREE: Press Command-T (PC: Control-T) to bring up the Free Transform function. You'll need to see the surrounding canvas area to add the proper amount of perspective effect. To do that, look near the bottom of the Toolbox. The second row of icons from the bottom has three icons, representing the three different screen modes. Click on the center icon and your image will now appear centered on a gray background that fills your monitor. Control-click (PC: Right-click) within the Free Transform bounding box, and a pop-up menu will appear with a list of transformations. Choose Perspective from the list, then grab the lower right-hand corner point and drag it to the right to create a perspective effect (as shown here).

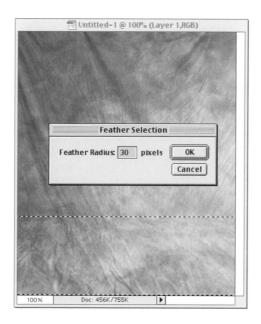

STEP FOUR: When the perspective effect looks about right (in other words, it looks like the background is bending where the floor would be), press Return (PC: Enter) to lock in your transformation. Now, go under the Select menu and choose Feather. When the Feather Selection dialog box appears, enter a Feather Radius of 30 pixels and click OK. (Note: for high-res, 300-ppi images, enter 55 pixels.)

QUICK TIPS

When you're in Free Transform, the keyboard shortcut for Perspective is Shift-Command-Option (PC: Shift-Control-Alt) and then click-and-drag a corner point.

STEP FIVE: The feathering you just added will soften the tonal transition we're going to apply in this step. First, go under the Select menu and choose Inverse (this changes the selection from the floor to the wall behind it). Go under the Image menu, under Adjust, and choose Levels. When the Levels dialog box appears, we're going to use it to darken the back wall. Grab the far left (black) Input Levels slider and drag it to the right a bit to darken the wall (here I dragged it to the right until it read 88 in the first Input Levels field). When it looks good to you, click OK.

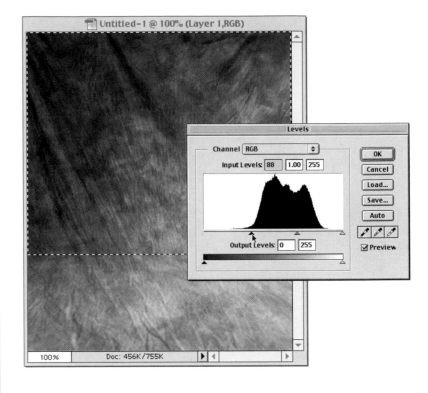

STEP SIX: Now that we've darkened the background, we'll lighten the floor by going under the Select menu and choosing Inverse again (this swaps the selection back to the floor). Go under the Image menu, under Adjust, and choose Levels. When the Levels dialog box appears, grab the far right (white) Input Levels slider and drag it to the left a bit to lighten the floor (here I dragged it to the left until it read 210 in the third Input Levels field). When it looks light enough to you, click OK.

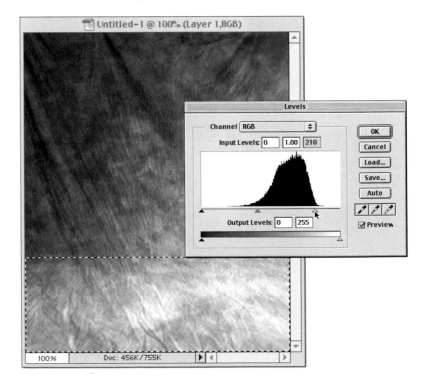

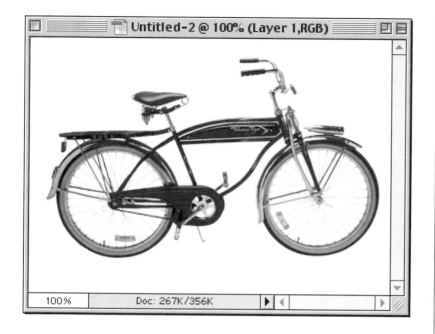

STEP SEVEN: Open the product shot you want to place over your backdrop image. In this example, the product was on a white background, so I clicked the Magic Wand tool once on the white background to select the background. Not all the areas were selected on the first try, so I held the Shift key, and clicked the Magic Wand again in the other unselected areas until I had the entire background selected. Then, I went under the Select menu and chose Inverse to swap the selection, which selects the product, rather than the background. (This is an old trick, based on the theory that it's usually easier to select the background, then inverse the selection, than it is to painstakingly select the product itself.)

STEP EIGHT: Press the "v" key to switch to the Move tool, click-and-drag the product shot onto the background image and position it on the background where you want it. Next, we'll add some shadows to make the shot look more realistic.

STEP NINE: We're just going to add two simple shadows below the tires, so we'll take the easy way out—we'll paint the shadow in. First, create a new blank layer by clicking on the New Layer icon at the bottom of the Layers palette. Make sure this new layer is beneath your object layer (in this case, it should be beneath the bike layer in the Layers palette). Press the "b" key to switch to the Paintbrush tool. In the Options Bar, choose a small, soft-edged brush that is about as wide as the tires are thick (I chose a 9-pixel brush). Lower the opacity to 40% so the shadow will be lighter, allowing the background under it to show through for a more realistic look.

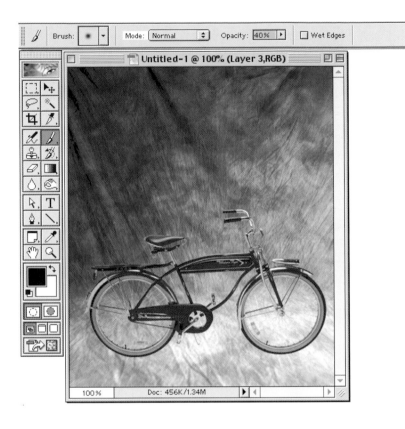

STEP TEN: The rest is easy, just paint a straight stroke under each tire, starting just to the left of where the tire touches the muslin backdrop and dragging to the right just past the center of the tire. Do the same for the other tire. Now, switch to the next smallest brush in the palette and drag another stroke directly under each tire, right where it meets the muslin. Lastly, to soften your shadows even more, go under the Filter menu, under Blur, and choose Gaussian Blur. When the dialog box appears, enter 2.5 pixels (for high-res, 300-ppi images, enter 5 or 6 pixels) and click OK to soften the shadows, giving you the effect shown here.

Creating Studio Portrait Backgrounds

This technique mimics a very popular background setup for headshots, but can also be used for product shots. This technique puts a nice glow around the subject's head and is ideal when trying to make an unattractive snapshot look like a studio portrait.

STEP ONE: Create a new blank document in RGB mode at 72 ppi (or higher, your choice). This is going to be a portrait background, so make the image taller than it is wide (as shown here). Press the letter "d" to reset your foreground/background colors to their defaults (black and white). Press the letter "g" to switch to the Gradient tool. Make sure that your gradient is set to Foreground to Background in the Options Bar and drag a gradient from the top of your image to the bottom, as shown here.

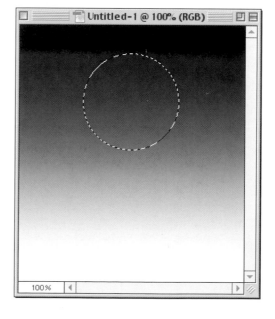

STEP TWO: Press Shift-M until the Elliptical Marquee (selection) tool appears in the upper left-hand spot in your Toolbox. With this tool, draw a circular selection approximately where you think the person's head might be when you add it later to the image (just get somewhat close, it doesn't have to be exact).

STEP THREE: Switch to Quick Mask mode by pressing the "q" key. Your circle will appear transparent, surrounded by a dark red to pink gradient. (Note: if it looks just the opposite of this—a red circle with transparent areas all around it, you just have the Quick Mask preferences set differently. To make it look like this, double-click on the Quick Mask icon below the Foreground/Background Color Swatches in the Toolbox. When the dialog box appears, for Color Indicates, choose Masked Areas, then click OK.)

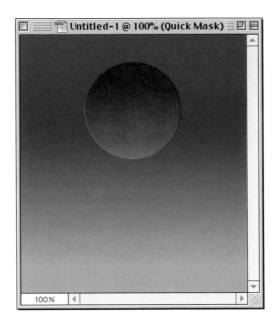

STEP FOUR: While you're in Quick Mask mode, you're going to add a large blur to this circle, so go under the Filter menu, under Blur, and choose Gaussian Blur. For Radius enter 25 to 30 pixels of blur (you can use between 50 and 60 for high-res, 300-ppi images), then click OK to apply the blur that later in this technique will appear as a soft spotlight cast onto the background.

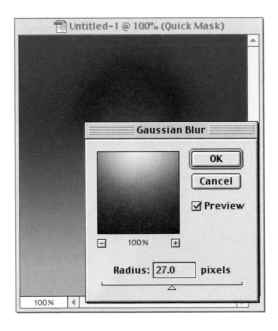

QUICK TIPS

Once you've created a color stop, you can copy that stop by holding the Option key (PC: Alt key) and dragging yourself a copy.

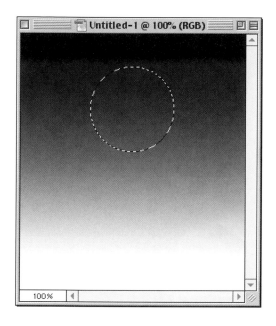

STEP FIVE: Press the "q" key again to leave Quick Mask mode and return to Standard mode. Don't let it freak you out that your selection looks just as it did before you went into Quick Mask mode—a round circle with no blur. In the next step, you'll bring the blur out.

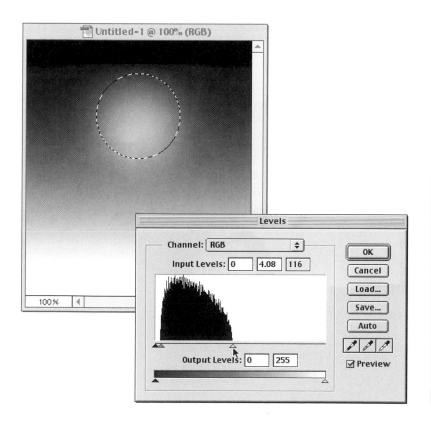

STEP SIX: Go under the Image menu, under Adjust, and choose Levels. When the Levels dialog box appears, grab the center Input Levels midtone slider (the gray one) and drag it almost all the way to the far left (as shown). Then grab the far right highlight Input Levels slider and drag it to the left until you reach the area where the Histogram begins (as shown lower left) to bring out the spotlight effect on the background. When it looks about right, click OK.

STEP SEVEN: Open the headshot you want to put on your portrait background. Using the selection tool of your choice (Magic Wand, Lasso, Pen tool, etc.), put a selection around the person you want to move onto your background.

STEP EIGHT: Press the letter "v" to switch to the Move tool, click-and-drag the image of the person onto the spotlight background image and position it so the soft spotlight glow appears behind the person's head with some of the glow extending out beyond their head.

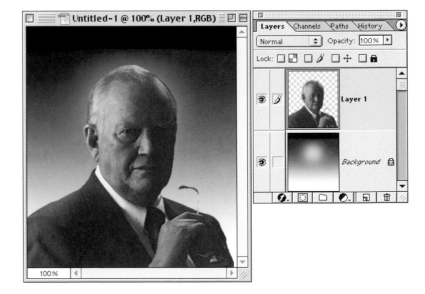

QUICK TIPS

You can position your layer pixel-by-pixel by switching to the Move tool and using the Arrow keys on your keyboard. Add the Shift key to move in larger increments.

STEP NINE: Click on the Background layer to make it active, and then go under the Image menu, under Adjust, and choose Hue/Saturation. When the dialog box appears, click on the Colorize checkbox that appears in the bottom right-hand corner of the dialog box. Next, use the Hue slider to dial in the color you'd like for your background (in this example, I chose a dark blue). Click OK to apply the color to your background.

STEP TEN: Once you click OK in the Hue/Saturation dialog box, you'll see the final effect. You may need to click on Layer 1 and reposition the person so the glow appears where it should (as shown here).

Adding Color as an Effect

This technique has been around for awhile, but what caught my attention lately is how effectively Gatorade® has been using it in their recent TV and print ads. They colorize sweat pouring from black-and-white images of sports images. Here's one example of how to accomplish this technique:

STEP ONE: Open the grayscale image that you want to apply the color effect to. Before you can add color to a grayscale image, you first have to convert your image into a color mode. Go under the Image menu, under Mode, and choose RGB Color. The image won't look any different, but now you're in a mode that will support having color added.

STEP TWO: Press the "L" key to switch to the Lasso tool, and draw a selection around the area that you want to add color (in this case, I drew a selection around the person's lips). Go under the Select menu and choose Feather. When the Feather dialog box appears, for Feather Radius choose 1 and click OK to soften the edges of your selection just a tiny bit (you won't see the softening on screen yet).

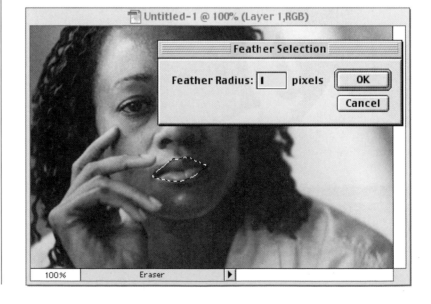

STEP THREE: Go to the Layers palette and, while your selection is still in place, click on the New Layer icon at the bottom of the palette. This creates a new blank layer. In the Toolbox, click on the Foreground Color Swatch and choose the color you want to introduce into your image (I chose a bright orange Gatorade-like color). Once you choose your color, press Option-Delete (PC: Alt-Backspace) to fill your selection with your foreground color (in this case, orange).

STEP FOUR: In the Layers palette, change the blend mode (from the pop-up menu at the top left of the palette) from Normal to Color to bring the color into your image. Press Command-D (PC: Control-D) to deselect and to see the final effect (shown here).

QUICK TIPS

Another way to add color to a grayscale image is to select the area, then go under the Image menu, under Adjust, and choose Hue/Saturation. Check the Colorize checkbox to color.

Depth of Field Effect

This traditional photography effect has been around almost as long as cameras themselves, but the effect is just now experiencing a rebirth in contemporary advertising and it's popping up just about everywhere. Here's how to create these depth of field effects in Photoshop.

STEP ONE: Open an image on which you want to apply a depth of field effect. This effect generally works best if the image is closely cropped and appears as if it were shot up close, nearly filling the entire image window.

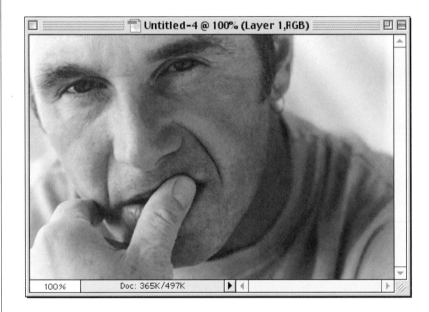

STEP TWO: Switch to Quick Mask mode by pressing the "q" key. Then switch to the Gradient tool by pressing the "g" key. Press the "d" key to reset your foreground and background colors to their default settings (black and white). Now, take the Gradient tool and click in your image, starting in the area you want to remain in focus, then drag toward the area you want to appear out of focus. Since you're in Quick Mask mode, you'll see a red to transparent gradient.

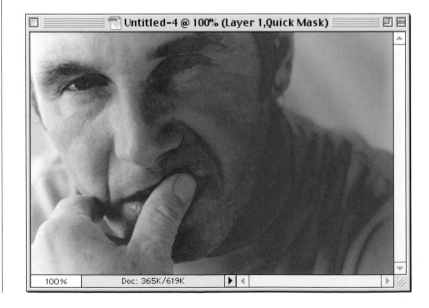

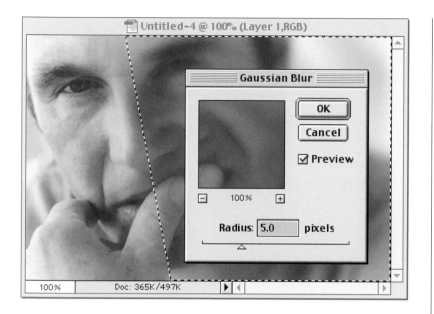

STEP THREE: Press the "q" key again to leave Quick Mask mode and return to Standard mode. When you do this, you'll see a selection appear on screen, primarily in the area where you want to apply the blur. Go under the Filter menu, under Blur, and choose Gaussian Blur. When the dialog box appears, enter the amount of blur you'd like for the farthest point away in your image, then click OK. Here, I chose 5 pixels. Don't deselect yet. Instead, go under the Select menu and choose Inverse so you've got the part of the image that's supposed to stay in focus selected.

STEP FOUR: Go under the Filter menu, under Sharpen, and choose Unsharp Mask. When the dialog box appears, enter 100 for Amount, 1 for Radius, and 3 for Threshold, then click OK to sharpen the part of the image closest to the person viewing it. Lastly, deselect by pressing Command-D (PC: Control-D) to reveal the final effect of having the image very sharp in front and, as it moves away from the viewer, smoothly changing to a blur.

QUICK TIPS

You can always tell if you're in Quick Mask mode by looking in the title bar of the active image window. If you're in Quick Mask mode, it will say "Quick Mask" after the name.

Adding Shadows for Drama

This is a very popular retouching technique for adding a dramatic effect, through the use of a lighting effect. This is especially popular in Hollywood, where it's often used in movie posters. The advantage for Hollywood is that they can combine headshots of the stars that were taken at different times, and then collage them together later with the dark side of each headshot used as a background for the next.

STEP ONE: Open an image where you want to add more drama. Press the "d" key to set your foreground color to black.

STEP TWO: Press the "q" key to switch to Quick Mask mode. Then press the "g" key to switch to the Gradient tool. Drag the Gradient tool from the center of the person's face to the edge of the image.

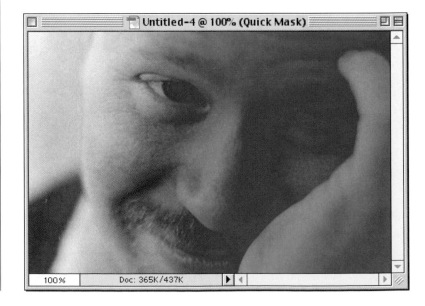

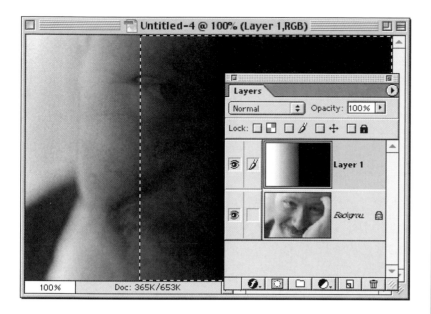

STEP THREE: Press the "q" key again to return to Standard mode. You'll see a selection appear on screen. If it's the side of the image you want to darken with shadows, go on to the next step. If the opposite side of the face is selected, go under the Select menu and choose Inverse to flip the selection to the other side. Create a new blank layer by clicking on the New Layer icon at the bottom of the Layers palette. Fill this layer with black by pressing Option-Delete (PC: Alt-Control) and then deselect by pressing Command-D (PC: Control-D).

STEP FOUR: In the Layers palette, change the blend mode of this black layer from Normal to Overlay and lower the Opacity to 70% (or adjust to taste). Press the "v" key to switch to the Move tool and drag this layer to the right until you like the amount of shading that falls on the face. Remember, you can tweak the position of the shadow and its opacity to get just the right effect.

QUICK TIPS

In the Levels dialog box, you can use the left Output Levels slider to lighten the overall image and the right Output Levels slider to darken the overall image.

INDEX

INDEX

PHOTO AND ILLUSTRATION CREDITS

Kalebra Kelby
Pages 32, 136, 154, 196

Dave Moser
Pages 24, 40, 126, 133, 157, 159, 161, 187, 200

Felix Nelson, Page 172

Jim Patterson
Pages 16, 26, 104, 112, 113, 134, 184

PhotoDisc (www.photodisc.com)
Pages 6, 10, 12, 36, 42, 46, 50, 52, 61, 72, 118, 120, 130, 138, 144, 162, 178, 192, 194, 202, 206 – 215, 226, 229, 234, 236, 238, 240, cover

Jim Workman
Pages 28, 54, 60, 68, 76, 78, 80, 82, 83, 84, 86, 90, 94, 140, 148, 216, 220

COLOPHON

The book was produced by the author and his design team using all Macintosh computers, including a Power Mac G4 450-MHz, Power Mac G4 500-MHz, a Power Mac G4 Dual Processor 500-MHz, and an iMac. We use Radius and Apple Studio Display monitors.

Page layout was done using Adobe PageMaker 6.5 and Adobe InDesign 1.5. Scanning was done primarily on a UMAX PowerLook 1100 Firewire scanner. Our graphics server is a Power Mac G3, with a 60-GB LaCie external drive, and we burn our CDs to a Sony Spressa 12X CD-RW.

The opening paragraph of each technique is set in Adobe Minion at 9.5 points on 13 leading, with the Horizontal Scaling set to 95%. The headers for each technique are set in Helvetica Black at 14 points on 17 leading, with the Horizontal Scaling set to 95%. Body copy is set using Adobe MyriadMM_400 RG 600 NO at 9.5 points on 13 leading, with the Horizontal Scaling set to 95%..

Screen captures were made with Snapz Pro at 72 ppi and were placed and sized within Adobe PageMaker 6.5. The book was output at 150 line screen, and all in-house printing was done using a Xerox Phaser 850 DX.

ADDITIONAL PHOTOSHOP RESOURCES

National Association of Photoshop Professionals (NAPP)
The industry trade association for Adobe® Photoshop® users, and the world's leading resource for Photoshop training, education, and news.

http://www.photoshopuser.com

KW Computer Training Videos
Scott Kelby is featured in a series of 18 Photoshop training videos, each on a particular Photoshop topic, available from KW Computer Training. Visit the Web site or call 727-733-6225 for orders or more information.

http://www.photoshopvideos.com

PlanetPhotoshop.com
"The Ultimate Photoshop Site" features Photoshop news, tutorials, reviews, and articles posted daily. The site also contains the Web's most up-to-date resource on other Photoshop-related Web sites and information.

http://www.planetphotoshop.com

Down & Dirty Tricks
Scott is also author of the bestselling book *Photoshop 6.0 Down & Dirty Tricks* and the book's companion Web site has all the info on the book, which is also available at bookstores around the country.

http://www.downanddirtytricks.com

Adobe Photoshop Seminar Tour
See Scott live at the Adobe Photoshop Seminar Tour, the nation's most popular Photoshop seminars. For upcoming tour dates and class schedules, visit the tour Web site.

http://www.photoshopseminars.com

Mac Design Magazine
"The Graphics Magazine for Macintosh Users" is a tutorial-based print magazine with how-to columns on Photoshop, Illustrator, QuarkXPress, Dreamweaver, GoLive, Flash, and more. It's also packed with Photoshop tips, tricks, and shortcuts for your favorite graphics applications.

http://www.macdesignonline.com

PhotoshopWorld
The annual convention for Adobe Photoshop users, it has now become the largest Photoshop-only event in the world. Scott Kelby is technical chair and education director for the event, as well as one of the instructors.

http://www.PhotoshopWorld.com

Photohop Photo-Retouching Secrets
This book's companion Web site features downloadable source files for many of the projects presented in this book. There's also contact info for the author and other important news and updates regarding this book and Photoshop retouching.

http://www.photoretouchingsecrets.com

Photoshop Hall of Fame
Created to honor and recognize those individuals whose contribution to the art and business of Adobe Photoshop has had a major impact on the application or the Photoshop community itself.

http://www.photoshophalloffame.com

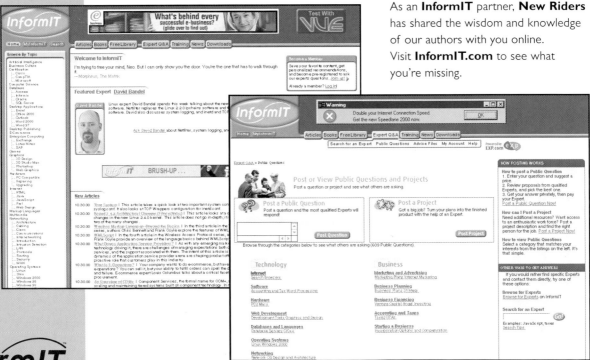